Many ~

B
L
E
S
S
I
N
G
S

to you. Walk
with Jesus.

Phyllis Highfill
3-10-19

To Marie

BLESSINGS

Phyllis Ann Highfill

XULON PRESS

FOREWORD

❧

On June 8, 2007, the Lord showed me to start sending daily emails speaking blessings over all my children, grandchildren, great-grandchildren, my sister and her son and family, and all the members of our extended families. Thus began the substance of this book.

Somehow out of the ashes of a broken life with many disastrous events, God raised up this voice to speak what He put in my mouth.

Having failed God in so many ways, failed my family in all the major areas of life, and being the cause of so much heartache, the idea of speaking blessings over their lives every day was one of the most refreshing words that could have been said to me by the Lord. Blessings are heard in heaven when you speak them. To declare words of blessing over our children, their husband/wife, family, over anyone, is to breathe new life over them. The blessings are heard by God, and He sets in motion a perpetual movement over the ones you bless. Your words are creative and to speak blessings over someone is like creating an atmosphere that God inhabits. Blessings are powerful and bring restoration to families. All blessings in this book were sealed with the Name of Jesus. (Colossians 3:17)

"And he shall turn the heart of the fathers to the children, and the heart of the children to their fathers, lest I come and smite the earth with a curse." Malachi 4:6

God says, "So shall my word be that goeth forth out of my mouth: it shall not return unto me void, but it shall accomplish that which I please, and it shall prosper in the thing whereto I sent it." Isaiah 55:11

"And all thy children shall be taught of the Lord; and great shall be the peace of thy children." Isaiah 54:13

"Many of life's failures are experienced by people who did not realize how close they were to success when they gave up." Thomas Edison

P.A.T.H.

Dallas, Texas

TO
ALL MY CHILDREN, GRANDCHILDREN,
GREAT-GRANDCHILDREN,
SISTER, NEPHEW AND FAMILY,
AND ALL OUR EXTENDED FAMILIES,

I CARRY YOU IN MY HEART OF LOVE.
FOREVER WILL I LOVE YOU.

"And the Lord answered me, and said, Write the vision,
and make it plain upon tables, that he may run that readeth it."
Habakkuk 2:2

"Write thee all the words that I have spoken unto thee in a book."
Jeremiah 30:2

"This people have I formed for myself; they shall show
forth my praise."
Isaiah 43:21

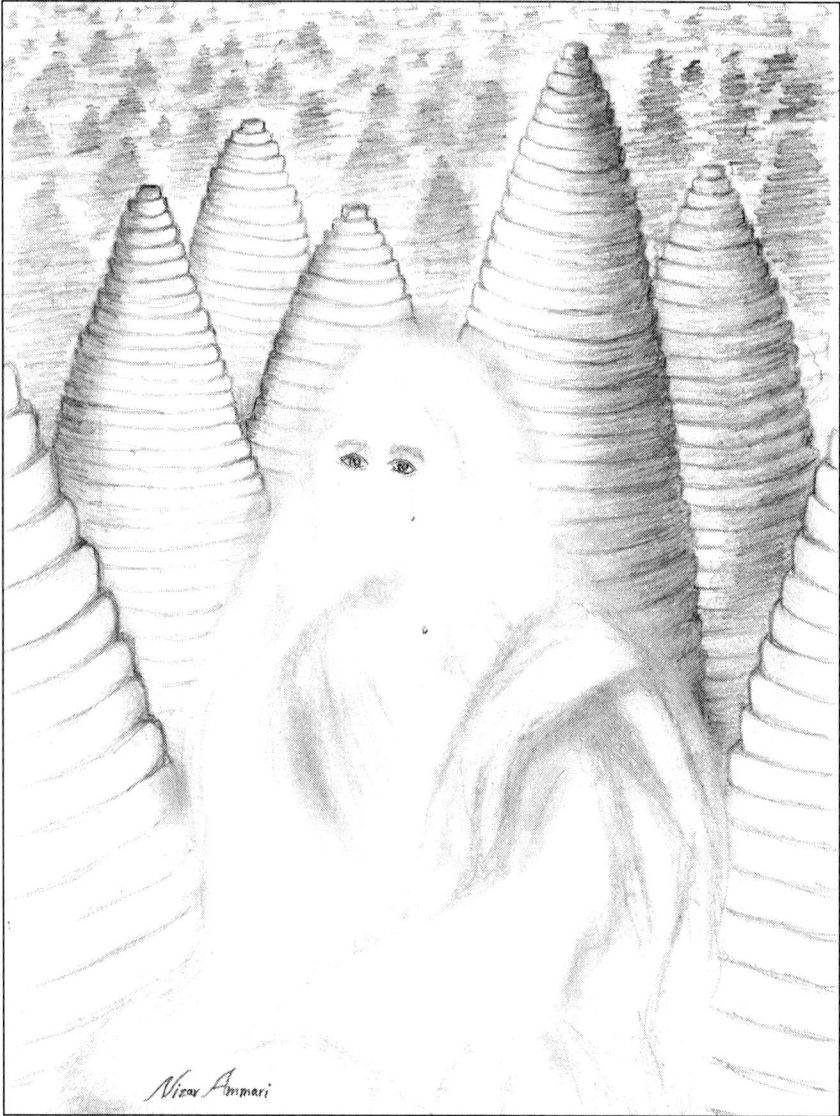

THE VISION EXPLAINED

One day while praying, I saw the face of Jesus. He was surrounded by eight cone-shaped stacks of gold coins, each coin representing a blessing. There were different heights of cones. The ones that were immediately around Him were three feet high and graduated up to seven feet high. As I looked closer at His face, I noticed that He had tears in His eyes, and asked Him, "What is it, Lord. What are you saying?" He looked off into the distance for a moment and looked back making eye contact and said, "All these are My blessings that are stored up in heaven to give to all my people but there are so few who are asking." As I watched Him, there was a tear that fell from his left eye onto His chest." He then revealed to me the weight of the deep sadness in His heart and the grief that so few are remembering Him. After He spoke, I saw in the distance behind Him, endless blessings stacked everywhere and all of them reserved for those who will ask Him.

The next day He said, "Put all the daily blessings that have gone out to your family in a book," and He spoke Malachi 4:6, Isaiah 55:11 and Isaiah 54:13.

This encounter gave birth to this book.

THE BLOOD OF JESUS

All the blessings that you will ever experience come because Jesus died on a cross for you and through Him you have abundant life and glorious blessings.

"For this is My blood of the new testament, which is shed for many for the remission of sins." Matthew 26:28

"And this is the will of Him that sent Me; that everyone which seeth the Son, and believeth on Him, may have everlasting life: and I will raise him up at the last day." John 6:40

There would be no life in the world if Jesus had not died on the cross and shed His blood for the remission of our sins.
"It is the Spirit that quickeneth; the flesh profiteth nothing: the words that I speak unto you, they are spirit, and they are life." John 6:63

The blood of Jesus reminds the hordes of hell of their eternal destiny. The evil one hates the blood of Jesus because that is what defeated him eternally.

"Blotting out the handwriting of ordinances that was against us, which was contrary to us, and took it out of the way, nailing it to His cross. And having spoiled principalities and powers, He made a show of them openly, triumphing over them in it." Colossians 2:14-15

Jesus' blood that was shed on the cross is so powerful that the souls of every person that believes on Him is saved. They pass from death into eternal life and will spend eternity in heaven. Every sin is forgiven through His blood when we ask for forgiveness. Through His blood our bodies are healed from the top of our head to the souls of our feet. Through His blood we are given abundant life. Through Jesus' blood Lucifer and all his myriad of angels who are termed "evil spirits" were defeated at the cross. Sin has no power over you. All who believe in Him from Adam to the last man born on the earth will experience salvation. Old things are passed away and behold all things become new. His blood is all-powerful.

My prayer is that you find Jesus as Savior of your soul. In Jesus Name.

A MOTHER'S LOVE

By Alicia

Age Nine

MOTHERS COME FROM HEAVEN ABOVE,

TENDER, CARING, FILLED WITH LOVE.

MY MOTHER MEANS SO MUCH TO ME,

I CAN'T EXPRESS IT IN WORDS, YOU SEE.

BUT GOD ABOVE KNEW JUST WHAT TO SEND,

FOR A MOTHER'S LOVE WILL NEVER END.

BLESSING UPON BLESSING

For you to receive all that God has provided will require that you take action by faith and accept what He is giving to you. Simply reach out and receive it. His blessings are yours. May your heart hunger and thirst for an intimate relationship with Jesus. To receive this, you will no doubt be prompted to pray. Getting in touch with the Lord through prayer and spending time with Him will strengthen you to press forward and obtain that sweet, pure, one-on-one relationship. The Holy Spirit is given in answer to prayer. The best return on your time is to pray and see the results. Your prayers go up to God and His answers come back down to you. That is a thrilling, life-changing return on your time.

My prayer today is that Kirstie Ann-Lynette, David, Kevin, Lindsey, Kris and Lauren will be powerfully touched by the hand of Jesus, so much so that each one literally feel His touch. May your lives be surrounded by angels that will protect you and hold you close to the very center of God's perfect will. May your every thought and action be cleansed by the blood of Jesus, and through this cleansing you be made whole. God has great plans for you in His kingdom service. We pray this prayer for all my family, individually and collectively. In Jesus Name.

"And besought Him that they might only touch the hem of His garment, and as many as touched were made perfectly whole." Matthew 14:36

Father, reach out Your hand and touch Renee, Johnny, Phillip, Nathaniel, Debbie, DJ, Nizar, Alicia, Sarah, Hannah, Bon, Terry, Kay, Zack, Caleb, Joseph, Jacob, Tatum, Harper, Kate, Cindy, Rick and their family, and all our extended families. Strengthen them to move closer to God. We lift them up to You before Your throne in heaven, asking You to look upon them with holy, compassionate eyes, and impart Your blessings to walk under Your cloud of glory, wholly and completely held secure in Your presence. The foundation under their feet is the holy streets of gold through the blood of Jesus. It is Jesus and Jesus only. In Jesus Name.

CHRIST OUR HOPE

"Looking for that blessed hope, and the glorious appearing of the great God and our Savior Jesus Christ; Who gave Himself for us, that He might redeem us from all iniquity, and purify unto Himself a peculiar people, zealous of good works." Titus 2:13-14

May the Lord bless you with the truth that your God is a God of hope. He wants you never to give up to any situation that would cause you to miss the mark, for He is forever your strong refuge. May He bless you with encouragement and give you a full measure of hope today in your work and in your play. Remember this: hope is a gift to you from the Holy Spirit. God will fill you with joy and peace when you believe that He works all things together for your good and for His glory.

"And the peace of God, which passeth all understanding shall keep your hearts and minds through Christ Jesus." Philippians 4:7

Father, may Your sweet blessings flow over the lives of these precious people and guide them into all truth. In Jesus Name.

ISRAEL

The first mention of blessing in the Bible is in Genesis 12:2, where God made a covenant with Abraham to bless him.

"And I will make of thee a great nation, and I will bless thee, and make thy name great; and thou shalt be a blessing:"

Because of Abraham's faithfulness to obey God when He told Abram (Abraham) to get out of his country, and from his kindred, and from his father's house, unto a land that He would show him, which is Israel, God's covenant promise to Abraham says:

"And I will bless them that bless thee, and curse him that curseth thee: and in thee shall all families of the earth be blessed." Genesis 12:3

God gave the responsibility of spreading the knowledge of Him to Abraham and all his descendants. They were told to go throughout the world and tell about God's existence and expound upon all His mighty acts.

The world is therefore indebted to the Jewish people who are descendants of the patriarchal line of Abraham, Isaac and Jacob. We would have no knowledge of God without their obedience to spread the truth of who God is and tell us of His redemptive plan for mankind.

We are told that those who bless Israel and the Jewish people would be blessed and those who curse them would be cursed. This has surely been fulfilled throughout history since the time of Abraham.

Bless and curse not. In Jesus Name.

JUST ONE TASTE OF GLORY

The presence of the Lord is all around you. He has great plans for you. He has imparted talents and abilities into your very nature. His gifts are in you. If you need more, He will give more. He is the Great High Priest. His sufficiency is your sufficiency. Come up higher. Get closer to Him where you can hear His voice and understand His call. He is always calling you closer to him. Can you hear Him? Can you feel His closeness?

Are you hearing the revelation of goodness that He is showing you? This revelation is liberating. It sets you free. You are given a better understanding of God's nature in you. Christ in you is powerful. Everything you need is right there in your heart. It is Jesus who came into your heart when you believed and accepted Him as Savior. Never lose sight of who you are. You are clothed in the righteous apparel of Christ. Just as a child who is dressed in their pretty new clothes would not go and play in the dirt, so would you not play where your clothes would get dirty. It would distort your nature. You and dirt do not mix, neither does oil mix with water.

God is calling you to arise and allow His anointing to break forth into your spirit. Turn from the beggarly elements of the world, discouragement, condemnation, fear, and those things the enemy is bringing against you. Turn and establish yourself today with a full heart and full assurance, believing that this wonderful God will do great and mighty works through you.

"For ye had compassion on me in my bonds, and took joyfully the spoiling of your goods, knowing in yourselves that ye have in heaven a better and an enduring substance. Cast not away therefore your confidence, which hath great recompense of reward." Hebrews 10:34-35

Oh God, open up the windows of heaven and pour into Your people great understanding, holy wisdom, deep knowledge, and God-given intelligence that will empower them to walk away from the dirt of this world and transcend them into the glorious world that You made for them to live. Feed them with a taste of Your glory. Let them taste it. They will never be the same. In Jesus Name.

GOD'S CHILDREN

"Now unto him that is able to do exceeding abundantly above all that we ask or think, according to the power that worketh in us." Ephesians 3:20

"Be ye therefore followers of God, as dear children;
And walk in love, as Christ also hath loves us, and hath given Himself for us an offering and a sacrifice to God for a sweet-smelling savor." Ephesians 5:1-2

You are sheltered in God, and no good thing will He withhold from them that walk uprightly in Him. You are on Jesus' team.

Within you dwells the Spirit of the Lord who made heaven and earth.

God rules over heaven and earth for you.

Within you dwells greatness. Christ in you your hope of glory.

Through Christ all things are possible and there is nothing too hard for Him to accomplish through you.

You can do all things through Christ who strengthens you.

In Him is all the fullness of God in His body.

So may you know the love of Christ, which passes knowledge, that you might be filled with all the fullness of God. Bless them, Father. In Jesus Name.

HOLY SPIRIT

"Now the lord is that spirit: and where the spirit of the lord is, there is liberty:

But we all, with open face beholding as in a glass the glory of the lord, are changed into the same image from glory to glory, even as by the spirit of the Lord." II Corinthians 3:17-18

May the Lord bless you with a full measure of the Holy Spirit of God for He is the One whom God sent to teach you all things, bring all things to your remembrance, show you things to come, guide you unto all truth, make you an able minister, testify to you of Jesus Christ, convict you of sin, help you with your problems, empower you to witness, release your inhibitions toward holiness, seal you until the day of redemption, strengthen your inner man, and give you eternal life.

May your heart be open to receive the Holy Spirit into your life, and all these blessings will be yours. Hold them close to Your heart, Lord.

"Peace I leave with you, My peace I give unto you: not as the world giveth, give I unto you, Let not your heart be troubled, neither let it be afraid." John 14:27

"And we know that all things work together for good to them that love God, to them who are the called according to His purpose." Romans 8:28

In Jesus Name.

FORGIVENESS

"In whom we have redemption though His blood, the forgiveness of sins, according to the riches of His grace." Ephesians 1:7

You are so blessed when you confess your sins to the Lord, remembering what Christ did on the cross of crucifixion for you, and you are forgiven. You yourself prove that He has forgiven you when you become the opposite of what you were. The old things pass away. They become worthless to you. There is nothing to be desired of the old life when you walked in sin. You are transformed by His blood.

After Jesus forgives you, His nature is placed in your heart . He gives you a spring to your step. You become alive in Him. The old ways which brought death to the good are gone. The Lord has raised you up. The new life will manifest itself in conscious repentance because the foundation of Christianity is repentance from dead works through the cross of Christ.

Now pass on God's forgiveness to others by forgiving all the people who have hurt you or wronged you in any way. By forgiving them, you are released from their control over your life. You become free from the wounds you suffered at their hands. You are free and healed. And the Lord steps into the picture to right all the wrongs, turning the bad into good.

"And we know that all things work together for good to them that love God, to them who are the called according to His purpose." Romans 8:28

Father, bless all these precious ones with sweetness of spirit, love in their hearts for others and a yielded life to You. Reveal the worth of what they have in Christ. In Jesus Name.

BELIEVER'S BLESSING

"Whereby are given unto us exceeding, great and precious promises: that by these ye might be partakers of the divine nature, having escaped the corruption that is in the world through lust." II Peter 1:4

"He that believeth on Me, as the scripture hath said, out of his belly shall flow rivers of living water." John 7:38

May the precious super-abounding love of Christ fill your soul. May you know the love of Christ, which passes knowledge, that you might be filled with all the fullness of God. That He would grant you according to the riches of His glory, to be strengthened with might by His Spirit in the inner man. That Christ may dwell in your hearts by faith; that you be rooted and grounded in love.

Father, communicate who You are to these precious ones by creating Your own nature in them and cleansing them from sin by your blood. The very same spiritual nature which is in You, Lord, is also in them.

Through the precious promises of the Word you are made partakers of His divine nature. He implants in your souls all those graces which are in His human nature. This is that new man, the new creation of Christ in you, that sinless nature, that spirit which is born of the Holy Spirit, that transformation in you into the image of Christ, that putting on of Christ, working His good works through you.

Oh bless them, Lord. In Jesus Name.

SURRENDER TO CHRIST

"Being confident of this very thing, that He which hath begun a good work in you will perform it until the day of Jesus Christ." Philippians 1:6

May you be filled with the fruits of righteousness, letting this mind be in you which was also in Christ Jesus, for it is God which works in you both to will and to do of His good pleasure, that you may be blameless and harmless and sincere, the sons of God, without rebuke or blemish in the midst of a crooked and perverse people, among whom you shine as lights in the world.

The most blessed you will ever be is when you yield your life to God.

"Likewise reckon ye also yourselves to be dead indeed unto sin, but alive unto God through Jesus Christ our Lord. Let not sin therefore reign in your mortal body, that ye should obey it in the lusts thereof. Neither yield ye your members as instruments of unrighteousness unto sin, but yield yourselves unto God, as those that are alive from the dead, and your members as instruments of righteousness unto God." Romans 6:11-13

Yielding to God brings righteousness and deliverance. So be marvelously blessed.

"But now being made free from sin, and become servants to God, ye have your fruit unto holiness, and the end everlasting life." Romans 6:22

In Jesus Name.

DID YOU JUST PASS JESUS?

If you were to cross paths with Jesus today, would you recognize Him? Would He stand out in the crowd that you would notice Him? Or are your eyes trained to see the glitzy, the beautiful, the appealing? Jesus was not pretty, nor was He appealing or attractive to look at. The Bible says he had no form nor comeliness, and when we shall see Him, there is no beauty that we should desire Him. There was no outward magnificence, ornament or splendor, beauty, excellency, glory, honor, majesty about Him. So He could walk by you without your noticing Him. He would not draw attention to Himself. Would you have known that you just passed the Man who would carry your sins to the cross so that by His blood you would have access to heaven throughout eternity? The Man who just passed by would take death off you and give you resurrection life, victorious life, eternal life.

What is inside Him - that was never noticed - is explosively powerful, captivating even. He is magnificence beyond human comprehension. The glory of God inside Him carried Him through the cross to resurrection life, and you were with Him. The greatness of His power to those who believe is in you. When He was raised from the dead, and God set Him at His own right hand in the heavenly places, He brought you with Him. Christ is in you and you are in Christ. That is your hope of glory.

"Far above all principality, and power, and might, and dominion, and every name that is named, not only in this world, but also in that which is to come. And hath put all things under His feet, and gave Him to be the head over all things to the church, which is His body, the fullness of Him that filleth all in all." Ephesians 1:21-23

You are blessed with blessings which come from heaven upon you. Jesus sees you as His child, His responsibility, and you are a son/daughter of righteousness to Him. You are surrounded with His love, peace, compassion and protection and though you were sometimes far off are brought near by the blood of Christ. In Jesus Name.

CREATED TO PRAISE THE LORD

"And the Lord shall make thee the head, and not the tail; and thou shalt be above only, and thou shalt not be beneath; if that thou hearken unto the commandments of the Lord thy God, which I command thee this day, to observe and to do them." Deuteronomy 28:13

May you be filled with the knowledge of His will in all wisdom and spiritual understanding. May you walk worthy of the Lord, being fruitful in every good work, and increasing in the knowledge of God. May you be strengthened with all might, according to His glorious power, unto all patience and long-suffering with joy. May you give thanks to the Father, which has made you fit to be partakers of the inheritance of the saints in light. God has delivered you from the power of darkness, and has translated you into the kingdom of Jesus, in whom you have been set free. You are redeemed and forgiven of all sins by the blood of Jesus.

May you be obedient to the Lord and walk in His ways so that He can establish you a holy people unto Himself. May you say from your heart, "I am going to ask God to help me in these circumstances until He pours new life into me so that I can be a blessing to all those around me."

When you obey the Lord, you will be bathed with His light. The old trials and problems will fall away under the hand of God who has power over all things. The Lord will lift you up. The Lord will give you freedom from the brash harshness of trouble you have been walking through. You will discover the genuine things that God will give you, the miraculous things that God will do in all your circumstances. You will suddenly look up and see that all the powerful promises of God are beginning to come to pass. People will gravitate to you because they see in you the glory of the Lord around your person. God is getting you ready for fulfillment of His promises because all the former troubles are forgotten. The former shall not be remembered.

"Therefore, "Arise shine, for thy light is come, and the glory of the Lord is risen upon thee." Isaiah 60:1

In Jesus Name.

HUMILITY

"If My people, which are called by My Name, shall humble themselves, and pray, and seek My face, and turn from their wicked ways; then will I hear from heaven, and will forgive their sin, and will heal their land." II Chronicles 7:14

May you have humility of heart and bring yourself into subjection to the Lord.

The Word of God is living. It is Jesus. You read the Word and in an invisible way, the presence of Jesus is imparted, moving over your mind, body, soul and spirit, giving you strength and stamina and new Life. His Life of holy magnetic resonance imaging is induced in you by His Holy Spirit and is working until Christ is formed in you.

"Likewise, ye younger, submit yourselves unto the elder, Yea, all of you be subject one to another, and be clothed with humility: for God resisteth the proud, and giveth grace to the humble.

Humble yourselves therefore under the mighty hand of God, that He may exalt you in due time." I Peter 5:5-6

"He must increase, but I must decrease." John 3:30

"He hath showed thee, O man, what is good; and what doth the Lord require of thee, but to do justly, and to love mercy, and to walk humbly with thy God." Micah 6:8

"But as He which hath called you is holy, so be ye holy in all manner of conversation:
Because it is written, 'Be ye holy; for I am holy.'" I Peter 1:15-16

May the God of all grace make you perfect, complete, establish, strengthen, and settle you. May you be blessed abundantly. In Jesus Name.

PRAISE

"For thus saith the high and lofty One that inhabiteth eternity, whose name is Holy; I dwell in the high and holy place, with him also that is of a contrite and humble spirit, to revive the spirit of the humble, and to revive the heart of the contrite ones." Isaiah 57:15

"Thou shalt also be a crown of glory in the hand of the Lord, and a royal diadem in the hand of thy God." Isaiah 62:3

May the high praises of God be in your mouth. May you praise the Lord for loving you and caring for you and overshadowing your life with His presence. The Lord is with you. He will never forsake you. His power is breaking evil off your life. He stands ready to defend you, to be a shelter for you, a strong tower that you can run into and be safe. He is a compassionate God. He holds you dear to His heart. He shall arise upon you and His glory shall be seen upon you. He is transforming your life to be more like Jesus.

He is listening for your call so that He can intervene in every area of your life. "You have not because you ask not." Let Him come in and restore everything that was lost for He repairs the broken and heals the heart. God knows your lack and your abundance and stands ready to fill to the top the cup held up to Him. Fill them, Lord, with your bountiful blessings. Anoint them with your Holy Spirit. Raise them to a new life in Christ.

May there be a resurgence of His life in you. The Lord will fill every void. He will be your personal shield who protects and covers you from injury or harm. Lord, we call forth angels to surround and protect these precious ones. May they be all righteous and may they inherit the good of the land. May you plant their feet on solid ground. May you be their everlasting light that dispels all darkness and may the days of their mourning be ended forever. Raise them up, Lord, raise them up and out of that which You do not desire for their lives. Give them peace, joy and happiness. Shower them,

Lord, with abundance, spiritually, financially, with perfect health, with intelligent minds, and revive their spirits to live in the overflow measure of God. In Jesus Name.

PICK UP YOUR BED AND WALK

"I press toward the mark for the prize of the high calling of God in Christ Jesus." Philippians 3:14

Father, we ask that You show these precious ones that You have so much more for them.

Greatness is within you. Hidden potential is inherent in you. It is the inheritance given you by God. It takes faith to obtain what God has for you, faith to believe unreservedly that what the Lord says, He will do. May the Lord find in you a yielded heart, a willing heart to be all that He wants you to be. Leadership and character go together. May you be a part of the army of the Lord that goes out and wins souls to Christ and that influences the people around you to hunger and thirst for righteousness. May they see Christ in you.

May you cry out to the Lord to give you the strength of the over-comer. May He anoint you with His Holy Spirit to press through and find the Lord standing and waiting for you to obtain all His wonderful promises that He has laid up to give you. May you desire to be just like Jesus, filled with love and compassion for a lost and dying world. May you be approved of God by miracles and wonders and signs, which the Lord will do through you. Jesus tells us to have that childlike faith that believes what is told them.

"He that followeth after righteousness and mercy findeth life, righteousness and honor." Proverbs 21:21

May the Lord protect you from the thief and robber. May your minds be filled with the peace of God. Everything God does is great and when you enter into His greatness, it is with humility and thankfulness that He loves you so much to save your life from the uselessness of a worldly life. To be greatly loved by the Lord is so wonderful. His love is your answer. He is the fullness of everything you need.

"I can do all things through Christ which strengtheneth me."
Philippians 4:13

In Jesus Name.

GOD'S LOVE

You cannot imagine how much He loves you. Only as the Holy Spirit brings revelation to your hearts can you comprehend His love. Nor can you grasp the joy Jesus feels when you talk to Him and include Him in your activities. May there be a continuous attitude of prayer going up to God as you go about your day. May you walk with Jesus. He is personally interested in everything, whether small or large, that happens in your life, not just sometimes when you think He is there, but all the time. There are so many blessings laid up for you in heaven that it would make you reel with excitement at the promises He wants to fulfill in your life.

It is said of Abraham that, "He staggered not at the promise of God through unbelief; but was strong in faith, giving glory to God; And being fully persuaded that, what He had promised, He was able also to perform. And therefore it was imputed to him for righteousness." Romans 4:20-22

By believing God, he and Sarah had Isaac at the age of 100 and 90, respectively. God counted Abraham to be righteous because he believed and did not doubt. May there be nothing that would rob you of the joy set before you. May the Lord stabilize your walk with Him. May you judge the good and the bad in your life and refuse to allow those things that are not of God to keep you from following after the good that God has for you. That which is not of God robs you of your peace. May you seek those things which bring peace.

"These things I have spoken unto you, that in Me ye might have peace. In the world ye shall have tribulation: but be of good cheer; I have overcome the world." John 16:33

"But glory, honor, and peace, to every man that worketh good." Romans 2:10

Jesus said, "Peace I leave with you, My peace I give unto you: not as the world giveth, give I unto you. Let not your heart be troubled, neither let it be afraid." John 14:27

In Jesus Name.

GOD HOLDS YOU

"For thou hast made him most blessed forever: thou hast made him exceeding glad with thy countenance. For the king trusteth in the Lord, and through the mercy of the Most High he shall not be moved." Psalm 21:6-7

Defeat is not in God's plan for you. You are safely held in the arms of the Lord.

We pray that you will submit yourselves to God. May you stand firm on the promises of the Lord knowing that he who believes shall obtain the promise. When God speaks He has something on His mind and when you listen and obey what He says, doors open for you to walk through into a whole new realm of His glory and into the glorious life that He has planned for you. The Lord is raising you up and you will not be cast down. Declare the Word of the Lord for it is truth and the truth will set you free. May you enter into God's peace and come out of the old into the new glorious life filled with all His blessings of goodness. May your bodies be cleansed and made pure as a child's by the blood of Jesus. May there be no abnormalities in your bodies for it is "by His stripes you were healed." I Peter 2:24

May God perform His marvelous miracles in your life. May you feel the strength of the Lord within you, guiding you, directing you, and lifting you up with His outstretched arms. May the things that entangled your life that seemed so important suddenly disappear. May the Lord walk among you to heal you, to help you, to raise you up, to enable you to see the things that are most important. Let all the useless dross fall away into oblivion. May you have the mind of Christ. May you think like He thinks. There is no sin in heaven. There is no darkness in heaven. There is no fear in heaven. There is no doubt or unbelief in heaven. There is no sickness in heaven. There are no diseases in heaven. No one is worried in heaven. There is no stress in heaven. May you be heavenly-minded and your mind associate with heavenly realities. May your life be linked with Jesus.

May your faith be solid and sound knowing that what you believe is the truth, the truth of God. There is no combatant against the Truth. Let the evil voices sound out as they will, but the truth will always stand. May the Lord work all things in your life after the counsel of His own will. In Jesus Name.

"That in the dispensation of the fullness of times He might gather together in one all things in Christ, both which are in heaven, and which are on earth; even in Him." Ephesians 1:10

GOD'S PROMISES

Father, may every blessing of happiness, contentment, love and joy come upon these precious ones. In Jesus Name.

"Blessed is he that considerth the poor: the Lord will deliver him in time of trouble. The Lord will preserve and protect him, and keep him alive; and he shall be blessed upon the earth: and thou wilt not deliver him unto the will of his enemies." Psalm 41:1

May the Lord command His loving-kindness in the daytime, and in the night His song shall be with you.

"O send out thy light and thy truth: let them lead me; let them bring me unto thy holy hill, and to thy tabernacles." Psalm 43:3

"Where no counsel is, the people fall: but in the multitude of counselors there is safety." Proverbs 11:14

"He that hath knowledge spareth his words; and a man of understanding is of an excellent spirit." Proverbs 17:27

"The name of the Lord is a strong tower: the righteous runneth into it, and is safe." Proverbs 18:10

Lord, stand guard over Your Word to perform it. May there be receptive hearts that are full of faith to believe every word You say. In Jesus Name.

INFLUENCE

While praying and asking the Lord how He wanted to bless you today, He spoke one word, "Influence." Wonder what the root meaning of "influence" is? and was amazed to find that "influences" is only mentioned in the Bible one time in Job 38:31, "Canst thou bind the sweet influences of Pleiades, or loose the bands of Orion?" Here we have bind and loose as the root meaning of influences. Pleiades means a cluster of seven stars (having sweet influences), or Orion (a constellation) meaning stupid, silliness, foolish, burly, fat (self-indulgence.) Bringing all that into the blessing, the Lord is saying that you have an influence upon everyone. The words in a book have influence. Every dot and tittle is important. If there is a typographical error, if it makes statements that are not true, the sweet influence is diluted. Every word in print carries with it influence, whether sweet or stupid. Your life is an open book read by all those who know you. The strength of influence means to bind or loose. Your influence binds itself to other people when they hear your words or see your actions. Words or actions will be loosed, and if stupid, silly, foolish or burly, that influence will affect someone. The influence will transfer from you to others and have a mental or emotional impact. Every dot and tittle in your own conduct will produce sweet or otherwise foolish influence. It is good to watch where you are walking. Evil will lead you to walk on stones of fire. God will lead you on a path where he will bind sweet influences upon every step you take.

"Deck thyself now with majesty and excellency; and array thyself with glory and beauty. Cast abroad the rage of thy wrath: and behold everyone that is proud, and abase him. Look on everyone that is proud and bring him low; and tread down the wicked in their place." Job 40:10-12

This scripture compels action. Deck thyself with majesty. Cast out rage and those who are proud. Tread down the wicked in their place. May the Almighty God of heaven clothe you with superior strength to actively put on majesty, excellency, glory and beauty. God, impart to them the focused, teeth-gritted determination that only warring angels possess, to cast off all garments that are ragged, torn, tattered, sullied, ugly, filthy, putrid and that carry the weight of iron. Cast them off in Jesus Name.

TOO HARD FOR THE LORD?

"And I WILL give them one heart, and I WILL put a new spirit within you; and I WILL take the stony heart out of their flesh, and WILL give them a heart of flesh:
"That they may walk in my statutes, and keep mine ordinances, and do them; and they shall be my people, and I WILL be their God." ·
Ezekiel 11:19-20 (author's emphasis)

May you experience miracles from the Lord. His miracles are yours. May this be the day you pull out all stops and wholly serve the Lord. May you allow God to turn your life around and wash away by His blood that which is unfruitful and unprofitable. May you submit all things unto Him and let Him help you work your way through any problem that seems to overwhelm you. He has the answer. He is the answer. May you encounter the Lord today in a new, refreshing, in a way that is life-giving. There is so much more of God that you can enjoy and that will enrich your lives. He is so great and His mercy and grace is extended to you. May you honor Him in your walk and talk.

Sin is usually the problem. Repentance is the answer that gives freedom and new life. The Lord is speaking kindly to you. He loves you and will do anything for you to bring you closer to Him. May you yield to Him.

In the Name of Jesus, let me plead with you not to waste your lives by being encumbered in worldly things that rob you from the beautiful, wonderful and glorious life God wants you to have. There were 35 wasted years in my life while God burned out pride, self-will, stubbornness, hatefulness, cruelty, and any other bad thing that comes with pride. "It is a fearful thing to fall into the hands of the living God." And I did fall into the hands of the living God and know the fierceness of His wrath against sin and self-will and pride. You do not want to experience it. God hates pride. And God does not tolerate pride in His blood-bought saved children.

"Of how much sorer punishment, suppose ye, shall he be thought worthy, who hath trodden under foot the Son of God, and hath counted the blood of the covenant, wherewith he was sanctified, an unholy thing, and hath done despite unto the Spirit of grace? For we know Him that hath said, Vengeance belongth to me, I will recompense saith the Lord. And again, The Lord shall judge His people." Hebrews 10:29-30

In Jesus Name.

YOUR STRONGEST TESTIMONY

"Because He hath set His love upon you, therefore WILL I deliver him: I WILL set him on high, because he hath known my name. He shall call upon me, and I WILL answer him: I WILL be with him in trouble; I WILL deliver him, and honor him. With long life WILL I satisfy him, and show him my salvation." Psalm 91:14-16 (author's emphasis)

The Lord holds your soul in life and will not let your feet be moved. You are on sound footing when you walk with the Lord. May the kindness and gentleness of the Lord sweep over your soul. May you be lifted up and encouraged by the Holy Spirit as you feel His strong arms around you. May you feel safe and protected in the loving-kindness and mercies of the Lord for He is faithful to never leave you nor forsake you. You are sealed with the Holy Spirit of promise. May the Lord visit you and guide you in His will.

"It is a good thing to give thanks unto the Lord, and to sing praises unto thy name, O Most High: to show forth thy loving-kindness in the morning, and thy faithfulness every night." Psalm 92:1-2

"Blessed be the God and Father of our Lord Jesus Christ, who has blessed us with all spiritual blessings in heavenly places in Christ: According as He hath chosen you in Him before the foundation of the world, that you should be holy and without blame before Him in love." Ephesians 1:3-4

Father, work all things after the counsel of Your will and break every hindering force from off their lives that they may experience a freedom to live life to the fullest. In Jesus Name.

HAPPY IS THAT PEOPLE

"How precious also are thy thoughts unto me, O God! How great is the sum of them!" Psalm 139:17

May you be powerfully blessed by the Lord who is your strength, your goodness, your high tower, your deliverer, your liberator, your shield and protector, who subdues your enemies under you, who teaches you to be industrious, who teaches you to do His will, who leads you in uprightness. It is the Lord who gives you wisdom and prudence to find out knowledge of witty inventions. It is the Lord who delivers you from poverty and causes you to prosper that your garners may be full, affording all manner of store where there is no lack. It is the Lord who will always supply every need that you have. You are His and He will never fail you.

"Teach me to do thy will; for thou art my God: thy Spirit is good; lead me into the land of uprightness." Psalm 143:10

"That the God of our Lord Jesus Christ, the Father of glory, may give unto you the spirit of wisdom and revelation in the knowledge of Him:

"The eyes of your understanding being enlightened; that you may know what is the hope of His calling, and what the riches of the glory of His inheritance in the saints.

"And what is the exceeding greatness of His power to us-ward who believe, according to the working of His mighty power,
"Which He wrought in Christ, when He raised Him from the dead, and set Him at His own right hand in the heavenly places." Ephesians 1:17-20

This is the greatest power exhibited in the Bible, when God raised Christ from the dead.

My Father, watch over and guide these precious ones that Christ may dwell in their hearts by faith, that they be rooted and grounded in love. In Jesus Name.

GOD IS LOVE

"Love doeth not behave itself unseemly, seeketh not her own, is not easily provoked, thinketh no evil. Love never fails." I Corinthians 13:5, 8

The entire world was created on love. God is love. Love is the foundation of life. Where God is there is love. It is the strongest force in the world. Love creates peace. Love brings fulfillment to life's deepest need. Love conquers. God tells us to love our neighbor as we love ourselves.

May your life be surrounded with those who love you. May you be blessed by the love of the Lord. May you be guided by the loving hands of God. May He fill your hearts with his love. Without love we are nothing. May your motivation be love. May you act and do because you love, and for this God will reward you a hundredfold. May everything you do be inspired by love. The Lord sees and will honor and bless your works and words. In Jesus Name.

"But God who is rich in mercy, for His great love wherewith He loved us. That in the ages to come He might show the exceeding riches of His grace in His kindness toward us through Christ Jesus." Ephesians 2:4, 7

"For thou art a holy people unto the Lord thy God: the Lord thy God hath chosen thee to be a special people unto Himself, above all people that are upon the face of the earth. But because the Lord loved you, and because He would keep the oath which He had sworn unto your fathers. Know therefore that the Lord thy God, He is God, the faithful God, which keepeth covenant and mercy with them that love Him and keep His commandments to a thousand generations." Deuteronomy 7:6, 8, 9

Father, stir up hearts to pray without ceasing, rejoicing that they are called by Your Name. May they not quench the Holy Spirit who is drawing them toward You. May they abstain from all appearance of evil. And may the very God of peace sanctify them wholly; and I pray God their whole spirit and soul and body be preserved blameless unto the coming of our Lord Jesus Christ. Faithful is He that has called you, who also will do it. In Jesus Name.

MORE FOR YOU

"I am my Beloved's, and His desire is toward me." Song of Solomon 7:10

May the winds of the Holy Spirit blow upon you and cause you to be a passionate worshipper of the Lord. May you be hungry for deeper levels of intimacy with Jesus. Angels are on the move releasing new anointing, new gifts, new promises, new ideas, and new favor. Miracles, signs, and wonders are on the increase. Divine ideas for supernatural prosperity and wisdom for witty inventions are bringing forth new businesses and even whole new industries. These are just some of God's blessings for you.

May the Lord get you ready to come into a dream-come-true super-natural existence, which God has always had in mind for you to experience. The barriers blocking you are going to fall away and disappear like the walls of Jericho. You will enter into a new realm of His shining glory and through you He will impart the full measure of His Heavenly inheritance, which He paid for on the Cross.

He longs for all His promises to become "Yes" and "Amen" for you, and the world around you as you reap a harvest of precious souls.

"Every man also to whom God hath given riches and wealth, and hath given him power to eat thereof, and to take his portion, and to rejoice in his labor; this is the gift of God." Ecclesiastes 5:19

My Father, move upon all these precious ones by your Holy Spirit and remove all the stumbling blocks out of their way so they can follow the Lord with full vigor of purpose. May they feel the Holy Spirit drawing them toward their divine destiny. In Jesus Name.

WELCOME THE LORD

"Ye that love the Lord, hate evil: he preserveth the souls of His saints; He delivers them out of the hand of the wicked. Light is sown for the righteous, and gladness for the upright in heart. Rejoice in the Lord, ye righteous ones; and give thanks at the remembrance of His holiness." Psalm 97:10-12

May you have the blessing of knowing that God loves you so much and is waiting to pour out His Spirit upon you. There is not a need that He will not meet. His heart is so tender toward you. May you stay quiet and let the Lord refresh your spirit and encourage your heart and give you a new beginning of seeing breakthroughs in all your circumstances. May the Lord bring deliverance and freedom where there has been hardness and harshness. May you be lifted up to live in peace mentally and emotionally. Lift up your eyes and see the Lord standing there reaching out to you and giving you abundant life.

May you block the way that intruders cannot steal from you. Resist the proud and the haughty. May the Lord enable you to take a stand against ungodly things that would weigh you down. Rise up and claim the Word of God for your life. Stand tall. Cast off the weights by giving them to Jesus. May you pray for God to control your thoughts and bring them under the subjection of the Lord. He wants to be your God, your provider, your encourager. May you see the glory of the Lord, and the excellency of your God.

Father, move on their behalf. Come close to them and may your presence stay upon them until they are brought out to complete victory in You. Lord, day by day cause their focus to be drawn to You. May they claim your promises without doubting. Give them miracles that their hearts may be awed by Your power. In Jesus Name.

GOD MUST BE FIRST

"The eyes of the Lord are upon the righteous, and His ears are open unto their cry." Psalm 34:15

"For the Word of the Lord is right, and all His works are done in truth." Psalm 33:4

May the Lord set in motion every blessing in the Word of God that He has spoken over your life. May every loss be restored with multiplied blessings. There is a new beginning now and God is going to do a new thing where the old cycles and the old habits will be replaced with the new. May you submit yourselves to the Holy Spirit who knows your heart and understands. May you enter in and possess all that God has in store for you. Just pray and reach out to Him.

"And I will strengthen them in the Lord; and they shall walk up and down in His name, saith the Lord." Zechariah 10:12

"Not by might, nor by power, but by My Spirit, saith the Lord of hosts." Zechariah 4:6

Father, may a host of angels be released to minister to these precious ones and bring them out of all that weakens them spiritually. Make them strong, spiritually strong, in the Lord. Revive their spirits. Restore all that has been taken from them. Show them how much you love them. Speak to them by Your Holy Spirit and give them ears to hear and hearts to receive the wonderful blessings that you have for them. In Jesus Name.

YOUR SURE FOUNDATION

"And now, O Lord God, the Word that thou hast spoken concerning thy servant, and concerning his house, establish it forever, and do as thou hast said. And let thy name be magnified forever, saying, The Lord of hosts is the God over His people: and let the house of thy servant David be established before thee.

"Therefore now let it please thee to bless the house of thy servant, that it may continue forever before thee: for thou, O Lord God, hast spoken it: and with thy blessing let the house of thy servant be blessed forever." II Samuel 7:25, 26, 29

"But let the righteous be glad; let them rejoice before God: yea, let them exceedingly rejoice." Psalm 68:3

"Blessed be the Lord, who daily loadeth us with benefits, even the God of our salvation." Psalm 68:19

The Lord shall establish you forever. You shall be taught of the Lord to walk in truth and to revere His Name, for great is His mercy toward you. Righteousness go before you and the Lord shall direct your way.

"For the Lord God is a sun and shield: the Lord will give grace and glory: no good thing will He withhold from them that walk uprightly. O Lord of hosts, blessed is the man that trusteth in thee." Psalm 84:11-12

My Father, lead them in godliness that their hearts be drawn to You. Establish their lives on a solid foundation that they receive the glorious inheritance that you have for them. Set their feet on solid ground. Surround them with the love of God. Keep them under the shadow of your wings and protect them from all harm. Reverse all the enemy's plans and drive them out. In Jesus Name.

GREAT THINGS IN GOD

"Who is he that overcometh the world, but he that believeth that Jesus is the Son of God?" I John 5:5

Father, there is a whole new world of blessings that You want to pour out. There are revelations of things important that You desire to give to them. There are easier ways to handle many situations in their lives that You want to show them. May Your will be done, My Father. We ask that You dispel all darkness by sending them light, the light of Christ. Send forth angels to minister to them. May they overcome all temptation and follow the Lord with a willing heart. Give them desires toward pursuing God's best. In Jesus Name.

May the Lord take the difficult things and make them simple. May you realize that you are building an inheritance every minute of every day that is being laid up for you in heaven when you meet Jesus. You are building with either gold, silver and precious stones or the reverse of that is hay, wood and stubble. Every action, every word, every thought is contributing continually to your inheritance in heaven.

What will you build with today? Gold, silver, precious stones or hay, wood and stubble? The things you do to conform to righteousness will be gold, silver and precious stones. The things that are of the world, the useless things, the sinful things, these are the hay, wood and stubble and will be wasted and will not merit a reward in heaven.

May the Lord give you eyes to notice every act, word and thought today. May you realize that every choice you make is so important. It is your God that wants you to have the very best here on earth so you can inherit the very best reward in heaven and be able to live throughout eternity in close proximity to Jesus and not simply waving palms forever and ever. May you yield totally to the Lord and let Him be mighty in you. May your faces glow with the radiance of His presence. In Jesus Name.

"I can do all things through Christ who strengthens me." Philippians 4:13

PRAYERS DEFEAT THE ENEMY

"Call unto me, and I will answer thee, and show thee great and mighty things, which thou knowest not." Jeremiah 33:3

Father, the one thing that moves You is prayer. It is amazing how the smallest or the greatest problem in life is simplified after prayer. To pray brings God's hand into it and there is no confusion or frustration where the Lord is. He brings calm in the storm, peace in the midst of chaos, love where a spirit of hate is. When He is invited into the situation, He smoothes out the rough places and pulls down mountains with the swiftness of His holy presence. There is nothing too hard for the Lord to take care of. He is the Almighty God and when we run to Him, we are safe. He pulls you into His secure haven where there is all-encompassing protection. To pray brings you into His presence where there is ultimate power to answer. In Jesus Name.

May you stand on this tremendously powerful promise:

"Behold, I WILL bring you health and cure, and I WILL cure them, and WILL reveal unto them the abundance of peace and truth.
"And I WILL cause the captivity of Judah and the captivity of Israel to return and WILL build them, as at the first.
"And I WILL cleanse them from all their iniquity, whereby they have sinned against me; and I WILL pardon all their iniquities, whereby they have sinned, and whereby they have transgressed against me.
"And it shall be to me a name of joy, a praise and an honor before all the nations of the earth, which shall hear all the good that I do unto them: and they shall fear and tremble for all the goodness and for all the prosperity that I procure unto it.
"The voice of joy, and the voice of gladness, the voice of the bridegroom, and the voice of the bride, the voice of them that shall say, Praise the Lord of hosts: for the Lord is good; for His mercy endureth forever: and of them that shall bring the sacrifice of praise into the house of the Lord. For I WILL cause to return the captivity

of the land,, as at the first, saith the Lord." (author's emphasis) Jeremiah 33:6-9, 11

GOD GOES BEFORE YOU

Father, You are forever watching for our eyes to be turned upward to You. May these look up so they will be enabled to stand strong in the Lord until You show them Your perfect plan for their life and Your peace fill them to capacity. May You, Lord, give them the excellency of power and knowledge of Christ. In Jesus Name.

"The people that do know their God shall be strong, and do exploits." Daniel 11:32

May the Lord give you revelatory comprehension of how He is leading you. May He give you a solid understanding of what He wants you to do, for He desires you to excel and grow strong in the knowledge of Him. May every day be filled with expectancy of how the Lord is going to work in your life. May the Holy Spirit guide you in the smallest matters as you see His hand in operation.

"Every valley shall be exalted, and every mountain and hill shall be made low: and the crooked shall be made straight, and the rough places plain: And the glory of the Lord shall be revealed, and all flesh shall see it together: for the mouth of the Lord hath spoken it." Isaiah 40:4-5

God has made a covenant with you that He would never leave you nor forsake you. All His promises are yea and amen. You can stand on His Word and believe by faith and you will see it fulfilled in your lives. God is faithful. What He says He will do. And there is no good thing that He will withhold from you as you seek Him and walk uprightly before Him.

Father, may all the blessings that are piled up in heaven for them come down upon their lives and they rejoice in the fact that God is a God of love and He desires to bless His people with multiplied blessings. In Jesus Name.

BATHED WITH LIGHT

"And let the beauty of the Lord our God be upon us: and establish thou the work of our hands upon us; yea, the work of our hands establish thou it." Psalm 90:17

Beauty means agreeableness, delight, suitableness, splendor, grace, pleasant, pleasantness.

The Lord will crown you with His goodness and lead you in paths that abound with the resources that are needed so that you get completely out of debt very soon. May you set your goals high, and accomplish them as the Lord gives you wisdom and knowledge and understanding of the times and seasons. May you not hear the voice of strangers but hear only the voice of God and what He is directing you to do. There is sufficiency in the Lord where nothing in your life has lack. The Lord will guide you with His counsel.

"If thou return to the Almighty, thou shalt be built up, thou shalt put away iniquity far from thy tabernacles. Then shalt thou lay up gold as dust, and the gold of Ophir as the stones of the brooks. Yea, the Almighty shall be thy defense, and thou shalt have plenty of silver. For then shalt thou have thy delight in the Almighty, and shalt lift up thy face unto God. Thou shalt make thy prayer unto Him, and He shall hear thee, and thou shalt pay thy vows. Thou shalt also decree a thing, and it shall be established unto thee: and the light shall shine upon thy ways." Job 22:23-28

My Father, establish the will of God in their lives. Lord, you say in Your Word that whatsoever we shall ask in Your Name, You will do it, that the Father may be glorified in the Son. We ask that all these blessings come upon them.

In Jesus Name.

SOLID IN GOD

Being faithful day in and day out without any affirmation from the world, is a powerful testimony of God's stability in you, and strongly indicates that your faithfulness is solid as a rock. You are immovable no matter what other people do. You are put in a place where you are sustained by the living God of heaven. Your connection is a lifeline between Jesus and you. You will not always feel movement in the line between the two of you, but be assured that the Lord has not moved nor has He lost connection.

As you grow in the grace and knowledge of the God, His face beams with approval. Your inner character is being strengthened continuously. His hand is holding the line forever. Be encouraged that the Lord has found you worthy of His continuous touch. He is preparing you for greatness. He is removing all your weaknesses and is pouring in heavenly blessings that endure.

"Children in whom was no blemish, but well-favored, and skillful in all wisdom, and cunning in knowledge, and understanding science, and such as had ability in them to stand in the king's palace." Daniel 1:4

"And in all matters of wisdom and understanding, that the king inquired of them, he found them ten times better than all the magicians and astrologers that were in all his realm." Daniel 1:20

God is raising you above the worldly things and bringing you into the promotion that He has spoken. He rules over all and gives promotion to whomsoever He will. Be blessed with the blessings of heaven and anointed with the power of the Holy Spirit to excel in all that He gives you to do. In Jesus Name.

HAVE FAITH IN GOD

God is standing right beside you to help guide you through every step in your life. "All things are possible to them that believe," Jesus said.

The simplest, yet most profound truth, is found in Mark 11:22, which reads, "Have faith in God." May this truth grip your heart, mind and conscience and propel you into a new awakening. This will lead you into a life of having miracles happen all around you. Nothing shall be withheld from you as you walk every day with the Lord and "Have faith in God."

Father, may they pray like Jesus prayed. He believed. He was faith in action. Jesus prayed with authority. "Be healed." "Storm be still." "Lazarus, come forth." "Daughter, thy faith has made thee whole." "Ask, and it shall be given you." "Seek, and you shall find." "Knock, and it shall be opened." Jesus spoke the word and it was so. May your words be "faith-filled. " In Jesus Name.

This day, let us decree and declare total healing for all our children, grandchildren, and families. "By His stripes you are healed." I Peter 2:24 In the Name of Jesus be totally healed physically, emotionally, mentally, psychologically. Psalm 107:20 tells us that God sent His Word and healed them. God's Word is spoken in Proverbs 4:22 as being medicine to all our flesh. God's Word is the most powerful medicine in the world and is capable of healing your body completely.

May He speak deep into your spirit and bring forth resurrection life. In Jesus Name.

WALK CONFIDENTLY

"And the prayer of faith shall save the sick, and the Lord shall raise him up; and if he have committed sins, they shall be forgiven him. "Confess your faults one to another, and pray one for another, that ye may be healed. The effectual fervent prayer of a righteous man availeth much." James 5:15

"Now unto Him that is able to do exceeding abundantly above all that we ask or think, according to the power that worketh in us." Ephesians 3:20

God will help you to be the person who puts his life in full touch with Jesus and then incessantly, insistently, believingly claims victory in Jesus' name. You are the person who the powers of darkness cannot withstand. Moral force defeats sin. The persistent praying of someone who is sold out to Jesus who has the Holy Spirit within them will drive out the enemy, and Jesus will give the victory every time, in everything you pray for. That is the effectual working of His power through you. May He bless you abundantly.

May God the Father of glory, give to you the spirit of wisdom and revelation in the knowledge of Him. He will reveal to your heart the love of Christ, which passes knowledge, that you might be filled with all the fullness of God. Allow Him to actively lead you through to the most marvelous times of your life. In Jesus Name.

PURITY OF GOD

"Draw nigh to God, and He will draw nigh to you." James 4:8

Prayer - secret, fervent, believing prayer - lies at the root of all personal godliness.

May your very soul long for the purity of God. It stills your soul and allows the peace of God, that only heaven knows, to settle over you. It produces the fruit of righteousness to be a way of life. You will desire nothing less than the purity of God to flow through you. There is a stillness in your spirit and a glow of Jesus that overtakes your mind and body and you live in sweet fellowship with the Lord. He becomes more real to you. The nature of Jesus is imparted to you and produces a quiet rest in your soul. Christ in you is your hope of a glorious life. May the Lord impart the desire for this blessing into your heart. In Jesus Name.

JESUS IS PEACE

"In all things showing yourself a pattern of good works: in doctrine showing uncorruptness, gravity, sincerity, sound speech, that cannot be condemned; that he that is of the contrary part may be ashamed, having no evil thing to say of you." Titus 2:7-8

God is constantly interacting with the earth, and it is the people who know their God that He moves through to keep a good balance in life. Choosing to live righteously stabilizes your own life but also the lives of those around you. You are a mighty force who holds to right living and allows the Lord to shine His light through you. May the blessings of God rest upon you. In Jesus Name.

"Blessed are the meek: for they shall inherit the earth.
"Blessed are they which do hunger and thirst after righteousness: for they shall be filled.
"Blessed are the merciful: for they shall obtain mercy.
"Blessed are the pure in heart: for they shall see God.
"Blessed are the peacemakers: for they shall be called the children of God.
"Ye are the light of the world. A city that is set on a hill cannot be hid.
"Let your light so shine before men, that they may see your good works, and glorify your Father which is in heaven." Matthew 5:5-9, 14, 16

ANSWERS TO PRAYERS

There is nothing more wonderful than praying and seeing the Lord answer your prayers. He has already answered prayers you have never prayed yet. He is waiting for you to ask. This connects you to heaven. Jesus is real. He is in heaven unceasingly making intercession for you. He is alive and desires for you to take root downward, and bear fruit upward in Him. He desires the very best for you, just as do earthly fathers desire the best for their children. You are a child of God and He is there to guide you into all truth.

The truth of the Word will set you free. Believe what the Bible says and watch doors fly open for you that you never realized were available. God is a mighty force moving in your behalf and there is no power that can resist Him. May your desire to please Him overcome all selfish, unfruitful desire. To become more like Jesus is the ultimate for your life and reaps heaven's best. You are wonderfully blessed. God is calling you to pursue this deep walk with the Lord.

"Finally, my brethren, be strong in the Lord, and in the power of His might.
"Put on the whole armor of God, that you may be able to stand against the wiles of the devil.
"For we wrestle not against flesh and blood, but against principalities, against powers, against the rulers of the darkness of this world, against spiritual wickedness in high places.
"Wherefore take unto you the whole armor of God, that ye may be able to withstand in the evil day, and having done all, to stand.
"Stand therefore, having your **loins** girt about with truth, and having on the **breastplate** of righteousness;
"And your **feet** shod with the preparation of the gospel of peace.
"Above all, taking the **shield** of faith wherewith you shall be able to quench all the fiery darts of the wicked.
"And take the **helmet** of salvation, and the **sword** of the Spirit, which is the Word of God;

"Praying always with all prayer and supplication in the Spirit, and **watching** thereunto with all perseverance and supplication for all saints." Ephesians 6:10-18

Pray for God to put on you this armor (spiritual clothing) every day. In Jesus Name.

BROUGHT OUT

The path to a victorious life as a Christian is to stop where you are and take note of where you are headed if you take the next step in that direction. If it does not lead you to walk with the Lord - STOP. Pray that God will help you to change directions. Choose the path of peace. Look to the future. Forget the past. Go forward. If you doubt, just keep walking toward Jesus. He will meet you in the path. Though your steps are unsteady and you are unsure of where the Lord's out-stretched hand is ask God to touch your eyes so you can see.

Take steps of faith. Believe without doubting.

Soon - and very soon - you will see the light at the end of the tunnel. You have been in the lion's den, but the Lord was there with you and the lions were unable to touch you. You have walked close to the edge, but the Lord stood in front of you and never let you go too close to the edge. Did you hear Him whisper to you that He was there? Or was there too much clamor in your mind that dulled the sound of His voice? It does not matter. He understood. He whispered that it was okay, because He will never let go. He is with you to the finish line and you will come out having been tried and tested, but purified.

"See ye have purified your souls in obeying the truth through the Spirit unto unfeigned love of the brethren, see that ye love one another with a pure heart fervently: Being born again, not of corruptible seed, but of incorruptible, by the Word of God, which liveth and abideth forever." I Peter 1:22-23

You are chosen of God, and precious, so that you should show forth the praises of God who called you out of darkness into His marvelous light. You will reflect the light of Christ more brightly than you ever thought possible. It is His privilege to take you where you are and make you a shining light for His glory. You are truly blessed. In Jesus Name.

BEAUTY OF JESUS IN YOU

"In the day that God created man, in the likeness of God made He him;
Male and female created He them; and blessed them, and called their name Adam, in the day when they were created." Genesis 5:1-2

"Thine hands have made me and fashioned me together round about." Job 10:8,
Psalm 119:73

Did you know that you are made in the likeness of God, and from the very beginning He placed a godly blessing on you which will never be lifted but remains on you still. He fashioned you and created you with His own hands. When you were being formed, His hand was on you. He has loved you before the foundation of the world. He put in you His sweet spirit. He gave you His pleasant and loving personality. He put laughter into your cells. He formed you as He touched every second of your growth. You are a beautiful creation of God. He put strength and stamina in you to stand tall for life's journey. When you were weak, He took notice and made you strong. He gave you eyes to see all of creation in the world He made for you to live in and enjoy. You are wonderfully made and the blessings of God are all over you. Believe it

Jesus takes you and puts you inside of him and Jesus is inside of you looking out.

The word "character" is not mentioned in the Bible. It means "the sum total of the distinguishing qualities of a person." God has made you perfect, but character is formed in you by moral excellence and personal strength. Character is developed by the choices you make. In Jesus Name.

"Blessed is the man whom thou choosest, and causest to approach unto thee, that he may dwell in thy courts; we shall be satisfied with the goodness of thy house, even of thy holy temple." Psalm 65:4

YOU ARE CHOSEN

"Show me thy ways, O Lord; teach me thy paths. Lead me in thy truth, and teach me: for thou art the God of my salvation; on thee do I wait all the day. All the paths of the Lord are mercy and truth unto such as keep His covenant and His testimonies."
Psalm 25:4, 5, 10

May the love of the Lord and His holy presence surround your life. You are chosen of the Lord to serve Him with all humility of mind and He will cause all things to contribute to His high calling upon your life. You are highly blessed.

You were chosen to win Christ as the Bridegroom of your soul from the foundation of the world. God will move heaven and hell for you to win Christ. Let the Lord go deep into your spirit and bring forth that which will glorify Him. The instant you grasp the truth of who you are in Christ, you will be so overwhelmed and excited that you will put every minute of your life to good use and not waste time on things that rob you. In Jesus Name.

"You are a chosen generation, a royal priesthood, a holy nation, God's own people; that you should show forth the praises of Him who has called you out of darkness into His marvelous light." Hebrews 2:9

HAPPIEST PLACE

"And whatever you do, do it heartily as to the Lord, and not to men; Knowing that of the Lord ye shall receive the reward of the inheritance: for ye serve the Lord Christ." Colossians 3:23-24

May the Lord bring many pleasant and unexpected blessings into your life. There is a world of good things that God wants to give you. He has abundance for you. He is personally interested in arranging well-ordered circumstances for you to enjoy so that His peaceful Holy Spirit is always with you bringing calmness and confidence to your heart. Even the things that may not matter much to you may mean that they matter a great deal to God. Nothing is frivolous with Him. You are a child of your Father in heaven and He is ever mindful of everything around you. Even your thoughts are of prime importance to the Lord.

"Your life is hid with Christ in God." Colossians 3:3

"And let the peace of God rule in your hearts, to the which also ye are called into one body; and be ye thankful." Colossians 3:15

May His peace overtake all your thoughts and bring you into His perfect will. May the Lord bring blessings upon you by giving your mind a complete rest and freedom from ungodly thoughts. May He bring you into the blessedness of having a renewed mind with clean and pure thoughts.

Whatever you think is what you will do. But God's ultimate goal is to transform the old thoughts that defeat you into new life-giving thoughts that are encouraging. Realize that Jesus set you free from all the old sinful life and has made you kings and priests unto His glory. Live the ultimate life for Him. In Jesus Name.

LOVE HAS A SOFT TOUCH

"Let all your things be done with charity." I Corinthians 16:14

How do you speak to someone with a broken heart? You speak in a still small voice because they cannot handle anything stronger. The Lord will give you His voice that is filled with His compassion and understanding and show you what to say and how to talk with love in your voice. His voice is filled with majesty and He will speak through you to the wounded and brokenhearted.

There is no substitute for love. God is love and when we come under His wings of love, we feel protected. There is such a strong force in the tenderness of love. You are in right standing with the Lord when you extend love to those around you. Love will replace self-ishness. Many wounds and hurts have been healed by the act of love. When the Lord takes over your heart and fills it with love, you have received the most valuable attribute known to man. For out of a heart of love will come all goodness, kindness and consideration. Love reaches out to touch those you love. Love is thoughtful.

May the Lord bless your life with love all around you. In Jesus Name.

"Charity suffers long, and is kind; charity envieth not;
Charity vaunteth not itself, is not puffed up,
Doth not behave itself unseemly, seeketh not her own, is not easily provoked, thinketh no evil;
Charity never faileth.
And now abideth faith, hope, charity, these three;
but the greatest of these is charity."
I Corinthians 13:4, 5, 8, 13

May the Lord pour His abundant love over your life and fill your heart with the knowledge that He will assist you to overcome all sin and bring you into His kingdom purposes. In Jesus Name.

GODLY SONS V. UNGODLY SONS

"I beseech you therefore, brethren, by the mercies of God, that ye present your bodies a living sacrifice, holy, and acceptable unto God, which is your reasonable service.
"And be not conformed to this world; but be ye transformed by the renewing of your mind, that you may prove what is that good, and acceptable, and perfect, will of God." Romans 12:1-2

You are not weak in the Lord, but are strong in the power of your God. You are bought with the price that Jesus paid with His life. You are of great value to the Lord. His love reached down and lifted you out of a life of sin and wasted years. He has a purpose for your life, a personal destiny that He has for you. No one but you can fill your place that God has chosen. You have a special gifting that God reserved just for you to enable you to fulfill what was reserved in heaven from the beginning. When once you start walking toward that goal, all heaven will open to assist you in keeping your appointment with God. Your reward in heaven will be great. May you be highly favored and blessed of the Lord. In Jesus Name.

KNOWING YOUR PURPOSE

"For God, who commanded the light to shine out of darkness, hath shined in our hearts, to give the light of the knowledge of the glory of God in the face of Jesus Christ.
But we have this treasure in earthen vessels, that the excellency of the power may be of God, and not of us." II Corinthians 4:6-7

May you be blessed of the Lord and secure with who you are and where you are. Each day brings new growth of character and purpose. God's hand on your life is there to strengthen you and help you to be an overcomer in all things. The Lord is daily making you more real. May you experience a new glow of God's light and love in your heart. May you always feel safe and warm with the Lord. He is forever overshadowing your life to bring out the very best for you. There are deeper depths and greater heights in God. He is the God of the mountain peaks and God of the most menial places in your life. He is your Lord. He is your light in every circumstance.

May the wonderful blessings come down from heaven upon your life and your mind suddenly clears so you can see what powerful miracles He is ready to do. The is the hope of the redeemed of the Lord. In Jesus Name.

LOVE RELATIONSHIP

Have a love relationship with God. That is profound. That would be the greatest blessing imaginable; to have a wonderful love relationship with God. And it is not impossible. When you draw near to God, He draws near to you. May this be the desire of your heart as you choose to believe by faith that you will have this relationship with God.

"But know that the Lord hath set apart him that is godly for Himself: the Lord will hear when you call unto Him. Stand in awe, and sin not: commune with your own heart upon your bed, and be still. Offer the sacrifices of righteousness, and put your trust in the Lord." Psalm 4:3-5

"For thou, Lord, wilt bless the righteous; with favor wilt thou compass him as with a shield." Psalm 5:12

Be abundantly blessed with the sweetest blessings from the Lord. May your actions and words point to Jesus so that you be a powerful witness for Him.
In Jesus Name.

NEVER FORGET

There is a lot of hustle and bustle in our world today, but all you need in order to get settled and find rest is to get quiet before the Lord and He will calm all things in your world and in your spirit. Jesus is your refuge. In Him is calmness and security. He is always watching over you. Your resting place is with the Lord.

The Bible says, "One sparrow shall not fall on the ground without your Father. But the very hairs of your head are all numbered. Fear ye not therefore, ye are of more value than many sparrows." Matthew 10:29-31

You are truly blessed. You have a very intricate God. He is detail-oriented. He knows all things about you, even the number of hairs on your head. His mind does not think in a realm of complicated, difficult, hard to understand, or entangled messes. He never asks why or what is going on. He is a God who is all-seeing, all-wise, all-knowing. He has infinite awareness and understanding and insight of everything. You have a God who is personally interested in all that concerns you and it is He who will lead you into His will where there is peace and rest in your soul.

May the Lord bless you as He has promised and lead you day by day into a closer walk with Him where you will have more and more blessings. In Jesus Name.

CLAIM AND BELIEVE

"Hear attentively the noise of His voice, and the sound that goeth out of His mouth." Job 37:2

"Is not God in the height of heaven? And the height of the stars, how high they are?" Job 22:12

"I have esteemed the words of His mouth more than my necessary food. Job 23:12

May you hunger and thirst for the Word of God, to read it, to be strengthened by it, to feel the love of God as you read it, to experience the blessings that God promises you, and to grow spiritually so that you become stronger and stronger in the Lord. The Word of God is your daily bread spiritually.

God's Word contained in your Bible is the most precious words ever written. These words are alive and as you read them, you receive life. They speak of everything - both in heaven and on earth. They are God speaking to mankind. The words in your Bible are anointed by the Holy Spirit. It is the only book that tells us the truth of what Jesus accomplished on the cross when He gave His life for us to be forgiven of sin and be able to live a holy life that pleases Him.

"Wherefore He is able also to save them to the uttermost that come unto God by Him, seeing He ever liveth to make intercession for them." Hebrews 7:25

"O the depth of the riches both of the wisdom and knowledge of God!" Romans 11:33

"For the Word of God is quick, and powerful, and sharper than any two-edged sword, piercing even to the dividing asunder of soul and spirit, and of the joints and marrow, and is a discerner of the thoughts and intents of the heart." Hebrews 4:12

In Jesus Name.

HOLY SPIRIT'S PRSENCE

When God breathes the breath of His Spirit, everyone knows He has come. Luke, the author of Acts, writes,

"Suddenly there came a sound from heaven as of a rushing mighty wind, and it filled all the house where they were sitting.
"And when there appeared unto them cloven tongues like as of fire, and it sat upon each of them.
"And they were all filled with the Holy Spirit, and began to speak with other tongues, as the Spirit gave them utterance." Acts 2:2-4

This "sound from heaven" was mighty and rushing, filling the whole atmosphere and all the 120 disciples present were filled with the Holy Spirit, and began speaking in another language. God has breathed upon you and equipped you to be bold in speaking the Word and living your life in obedience to Him. Everything that relates to God is powerful and will lovingly help you live above sin and alive unto God. Bless them, Lord.

"And when they had prayed, the place was shaken where they were assembled together; and they were all filled with the Holy Spirit, and they spoke the Word of God with boldness." Acts 4:31

When the presence of the Holy Spirit comes, things happen. He ignites the air with His holiness and things change. He puts fire in your bones and there is no stopping you from propelling toward the Lord with a new vigor. Suddenly you become more alive than you have ever been. Suddenly you are not the same person that you were. You are now alive unto God with a new anticipation and desire to thrust forward to new heights and deeper purpose in the Lord. God is for you. He is drawing you closer to Him. He wants you to fulfill your destiny, your call, the plans that He has for you. After you believed, you were sealed with that Holy Spirit of promise.

"In whom also we have obtained an inheritance, being predestined according to the purpose of Him who worketh all things after the counsel of His own will." Ephesians 1:11

May you be blessed, anointed, comforted and strengthened with the Holy Spirit of promise. In Jesus Name.

OVERCOMERS ARE RISING

"If my people, which are called by my name, shall humble themselves, and pray, and seek My face, and turn from their wicked ways; then will I hear from heaven, and will forgive their sin, and will heal their land." II Chronicles 7:14

May this day bring great peace to your hearts that God is the Lord over all. May you be filled with many "suddenly" experiences where you suddenly are taken up into a glory cloud with the Lord. May your hands not wax weak, may your heart be filled with continual joy, and your spirits lifted to greater planes with God.

There is an expectancy in the air. The Lord is walking among us and we are feeling His glorious presence in greater and greater dimensions. Today is a "no-holds-barred" day where the Lord walks through the barriers and restraints and makes a way where there is no way. Nothing can hold back the Lord. He is on the move to claim the land for Himself. May you experience new revelation and greater insight into the Word of God that will enlighten your minds to the deeper revelations of Him.

Today is the day the overcomers take the land. The overcomers are rising to the occasion and pulling down the forces of darkness in prayer and weaken their causes. We cry out to God and He hears us. He answers when we call out to Him.

Nothing shall move you. You are standing on the Rock Christ Jesus and in Him is no defeat. You are stable and secure in Him. You are protected from all evil. May the light of heaven rest upon your heads and fill you with His Holy Spirit. In Jesus Name.

WALK IN HOLINESS

When the Lord manifests Himself in your circumstances, He becomes a very real God of love.

"For with thee is the fountain of life: in thy light shall we see light. O continue thy loving-kindness unto them that know thee; and thy righteousness to the upright in heart." Psalm 36:9, 10

"Let us hold fast the profession of our faith without wavering: (for He is faithful that promised;) And let us consider one another to provoke unto love and to good works." Hebrews 10:23, 24

You are the ones whom the Lord has chosen to be His ambassadors here on earth. When you walk in holiness and righteousness you are clothed with the presence of the Lord. People's eyes will see the Spirit of the Lord on you though their eyes cannot actually see it, but they feel His presence. This in itself is a witness to the world. You carry a special bearing and connection with the Lord that is felt by those around you.

Moses had the glory of the Lord on his face that blinded the people and he had to cover his head when he came down after talking to the Lord 40 days and 40 nights on Mt. Sinai. When you carry the glory, you will never be aware of it, but by instinct you must always protect the anointing on your life and never let it be sullied by the filth of the world. God is very jealous of those who carry His anointed presence.

May the presence of the Lord become stronger and stronger as you yield yourself to Him. Be abundantly blessed. In Jesus Name.

ZEALOUS FOR GOD

"Mercy unto you, and peace and love be multiplied. Keep yourselves in the love of God, looking for the mercy of our Lord Jesus Christ unto eternal life." Jude 2, 21

Lord, we pray:

May you be zealous and spiritually fervent to serve the Lord. He will bring blessings to your homes and lives and reveal to you His awesome presence. May He give you a spirit of endurance and encouragement to follow Him. Jesus led a life of perfect balance, and He offers that to you every day. He accomplished everything God sent Him to do, and you can too. Yet He always found time to show love to everyone around Him. With a restful leisure, He spent time with them. People loved Him. Some hated Him. We can learn to live by His example. Watch where His footsteps are and follow Him and you will reap the most precious blessings possible.

Be wonderfully blessed. In Jesus Name.

VIRTUE AND VITALITY

God's ways are higher than our ways, and His thoughts are higher than our thoughts. He is all-wise and He still sits on His throne as God over all. In this you can take great comfort. This is His blessing.

His love is always directed toward you and is your covering and protection under all circumstances. Nothing escapes Him. He is full of compassion for you. He will never fall short of providing everything you need. He is a virtuous God with complete miraculous power, which is extended to you. Lord, bless these with this powerful provision.

We pray this over your life:

"Grace and peace be multiplied unto you through the knowledge of God, and of Jesus our Lord. According as His divine power hath given unto us all things that pertain unto life and godliness, through the knowledge of Him that hath called us to glory and virtue. Whereby are given unto us exceeding great and precious promises: that by these ye might be partakers of the divine nature, having escaped the corruption that is in the world through lust.

"And beside this, giving all diligence, add to your faith virtue; and to virtue knowledge;

"And to knowledge temperance; and to temperance patience; and to patience godliness;

"And to godliness brotherly kindness; and to brotherly kindness charity.

"For if these things be in you, and abound, they make you that ye shall neither be barren nor unfruitful in the knowledge of our Lord Jesus Christ." II Peter 1:3-8

May you press forward with a new-found fervency to know Jesus and experience His unlimited blessings every day of your life. He paid the price for you to be outstanding and accomplished as you obey Him without reservation. In Jesus Name.

TOWARD THE GOAL

Lord we pray:

May God in whose hand is your soul, and to whom all your ways belong, receive your love and honor today. May He become more and more important to you. May your heart be drawn to Him. When you find the Lord taking care of you in ways that go beyond human means, you will be filled with such an awe of Him that there will be no words to describe how wonderful and amazing He truly is. And the more active He is in your life, the more you will become acquainted with Him and be able to enjoy His incredible love and concern over every detail of your life. He is mindful of everything about you, past, present and future, and His touch brings total healing. In Jesus Name.

"And straightway all the people, when they beheld Him, were greatly amazed, and running to Him saluted Him." Mark 9:15

Oh how blessed are the people who know their God. Father touch them with Your Holy Spirit. In Jesus Name.

ENOCH WALKED WITH GOD

Getting into God's stride means that whether you are in the limelight, being the most-popular-guy-on-the-block, or tending to the common day-to-day things, you are being molded by the mighty hands of God in the least or the most important. He is constantly building character in you and making you the person who is pleasing to Him. He desires that you max out in spiritual growth. You are as vital in the small ordinary things as you are in the great out-in-front times. The Bible says, "Enoch walked with God." Genesis 5:22, 24. And then nothing else is said of him in Genesis. Yet he was such a godly, humble man that God "took" him and he was lifted up into heaven and never died. He and Elijah were the only ones who never died. You wonder why more was not said of Enoch since he was such a wonderful man but all God wanted to say of him was that "Enoch walked with Me." That was the most important thing God could say of him.

"The precious sons of Zion, comparable to fine gold, how are they esteemed as earthen pitchers, the work of the hands of the potter." Lamentations 4:2

You are as fine gold to the Lord. You are not some ordinary earthen pitcher made by a potter. You are fine gold, made by the hands of the living God and your worth is priceless. From God's standpoint, you are His chosen, His beloved. May you let Him fill your atmosphere wherever you are. Welcome Him. In Jesus Name.

GOD'S GRACE

My prayer is that:

God refresh these precious souls and give them a special talent that will be used for Your glory. Open up the windows of heaven and pour blessings of joy over their hearts. Help them to excel in that which You have given them to do. May they reach up and willingly take hold of Your hand to guide them through their day. Let favor fall into every crevice of their lives. Lift their hearts with encouragement and bring transformation in a miraculous way. Pull out all stops and hindrances and draw them up over the top. May they see the hand of God clearing out the impossible situations and creating an uncluttered path. Anoint them with Your Holy Spirit to stand tall and not be defeated. Give them thankful hearts to praise You for all Your mercy and grace that you have given them. In Jesus Name.

"For the Lord shall comfort Zion: He will comfort all her waste places: and He will make her wilderness like Eden, and her desert like the garden of the Lord; joy and gladness shall be found therein, thanksgiving, and the voice of melody.

I, even I am He that comforteth you." Isaiah 51:3, 12

God says that all things are possible to them who believe.

The Israelis say that nothing is impossible. It just takes a little longer. In Jesus Name.

DEVOTED TO GOD

"Thy vows are upon me, O God: I will render praises unto thee. For thou hast delivered my soul from death: wilt not thou deliver my feet from falling, that I may walk before God in the light of the living? Psalm 56:12-13

The miraculous is now at work. It has been long sought after and is now coming forth.

"Hear me, O Lord, for thy loving-kindness is good: turn unto me according to the multitude of thy tender mercies." Psalm 69:16

May the moral character of Jesus be imparted to you as you seek to walk with a high level of integrity. May you take every opportunity to live by this higher standard of righteousness. This will bring blessings upon you and those around you that will be refreshing to your heart, mind, soul, body and spirit. Your relationship with Jesus will become more precious because your mind is being renewed and revived. Be blessed and reach out and bless others also. In Jesus Name.

CHANGED FROM GLORY TO GLORY

"Now the Lord is that Spirit: and where the Spirit of the Lord is, there is liberty.

But we all, with open face beholding as in a glass the glory of the Lord, are changed into the same image from glory to glory, even as by the Spirit of the Lord. II Corinthians 3:17-18

The radiance of the glory of God is in the face of Jesus Christ. By being filled with the Holy Spirit you take on that same radiance and become a mirror of His own character. People see Jesus in you. Protecting that is so important. Try never to be so busy that you cannot maintain a good relationship with Him. By beholding as in a mirror the glory of the Lord, you are transformed from glory to glory to be like Him.

Just as a weightlifter adds more weight to the bar as his muscles become stronger, so the glory of the Lord is added to your inner man and spirit as you grow stronger spiritually.

The Lord gave me a vision one day. I saw myself walking up a ladder and He said, "The higher you go up spiritually, the more visible you are to the people watching you, and the more they will pop shot you." This has been very true.

Follow the Lord and live your life as unto Him. Be blessed. In Jesus Name.

PRAY GOD'S PURPOSES

"Likewise the Spirit also helpeth our infirmities; for we know not what we should pray for as we ought:: but the Spirit itself maketh intercession for us with groaning which cannot be uttered. And He that searcheth the hearts knoweth what is the mind of the Spirit, because He maketh intercession for the saints according to the will of God." Romans 8:26-27

Prayer takes you closer and closer to God. Prayer is not talking to God only. It is listening to the Holy Spirit's prompting and then talking. Let the Holy Spirit teach you how to pray. He understands praying perfectly. He is the Spirit of prayer. Quietly pray, "Holy Spirit, teach me how to pray," In Jesus Name. and He will. The highest law of the Christian life is obedience to the leading of the Holy Spirit. His leading always agrees with the Word of God. Prayer must be prayed In Jesus Name. The relationship of prayer is through Jesus.

"The effectual fervent prayer of a righteous man availeth much." James 5:16

"Be careful for nothing; but in everything by prayer and supplication with thanksgiving let your requests be made known unto God. And the peace of God, which passeth all understanding, shall keep your hearts and minds through Christ Jesus." Philippians 4:6-7

May you be perfected by maturity in Christ to be a channel of comfort and encouragement to others. Be blessed to be of one mind, live in peace; and the God of love and peace shall be with you. Be • wonderfully blessed, precious ones. In Jesus Name.

GOD'S ENDUEMENT OF POWER

"But this is that which was spoken by the prophet Joel;

And it shall come to pass in the last days, saith God, I will pour out of my Spirit upon all flesh: and your sons and your daughters shall prophesy, and your young men shall see visions, and your old men shall dream dreams: and on my servants and on My handmaidens I will pour out in those days of my Spirit: and they shall prophesy: and I will show wonders in heaven above, and signs in the earth beneath. And it shall come to pass, that whosoever shall call on the name of the Lord shall be saved." Acts 2:16, 17-19, 21

Lord, we pray that:
The Holy Spirit will open your hearts to hear these powerful words. They are glorious blessings of the Lord. Reach out and touch the Lord and by faith claim the fulfillment of all He has called you to do. You have a blessed destiny in God. The light of Christ in you is a powerful blessing to be used to enlighten the darkness that most people live in every day.

"Let your light so shine before men, that they may see your good works, and glorify your Father which is in heaven." Matthew 5:16

Jesus came, "To open their eyes, and to turn them from darkness to light, and from the power of satan unto God, that they may receive forgiveness of sins, and inheritance among them which are sanctified by faith that is in Me." Acts 26:18

When Jesus was on the earth, He was bold to cut through the unbelief and resistance that came upon Him by the enemy, as He preached the gospel of salvation. He spoke with authority as no other man has ever spoken. You are blessed to know Jesus. In Jesus Name.

THANKFUL YOU ARE CALLED

Everything that happens to you is molded into character, to make you solid as a rock, in mind, body, soul, spirit, and emotions. There is never a day wasted. God uses even the trash and the mundane to fuel in you a godliness that will one day burst forth and you will walk in ultimate dedication to Him. He is always forming greatness in you to bring you into the glorious relationship with Jesus that surpasses anything you could ever imagine. He is constantly bringing you closer to His presence.

The Highest Himself shall establish you. He is admonishing you to get wisdom, keep understanding, have knowledge to reap the blessing of loving your own soul, finding good, you will spare your words and have an excellent spirit. These are characteristics that will be developed in you. Ask Him to work all these into your character. These are blessings.

"The Highest Himself shall establish her. Psalm 87:5

"He that getteth wisdom loves his own soul: he that keepeth understanding shall find good." Proverbs 19:8

"He that hath knowledge spareth his words: and a man of understanding is of an excellent spirit." Proverbs 17:27

May God's blessings pour over your life and all that relates to you. May God send good things, glorious things into your life. In Jesus Name.

SARAH'S WITNESS

One day at the swimming pool, my granddaughter, Sarah decided she was going to baptize her sister, Hannah, in the pool. She raised her hand and said, "Hannah, I baptize you in the name of the Father, Son and Holy Spirit that you be raised to new life in Christ." She baptized her several times, eight maybe,, and it got the attention of everyone at the pool. It was quite amazing to watch because all the people had stopped and were listening and watching them.

Sometimes you never know when the Lord will use you to be a witness for Him and when He uses children who are so innocent and pure of heart, it is quite impressive.

"Go ye therefore, and teach all nations, baptizing them in the name of the Father, and of the Son, and of the Holy Spirit." Matthew 28:19

May the Holy Spirit move in your heart to be a strong witness in word and deed. In this manner, many are won to Christ and find Him as Savior of their souls. Be mightily blessed as you are led to tell others about Jesus. In Jesus Name.

NO ONE LIKE JESUS

Father, reach out and touch them. May the blessings of Jesus fall on you today and you walk in the strength of the Lord. May you feel His love and experience His wonderful grace and favor in every area of your life. He is the Lord and it is He who has promised to fill your heart with joy and peace and abundant life. Be blessed by His sweet spirit and holy presence.

"How excellent is thy loving-kindness, O God!
"Therefore the children of men put their trust under the shadow of thy wings.
"They shall be abundantly satisfied with the fatness of thy house; and thou shalt make them drink of the river of thy pleasures.
"For with thee is the fountain of life: in thy light shall we see light."
Psalm 36:7-9

Read again, if you will, what He says about the children of men. Pray it over yourself each morning and again before you go to sleep. Be blessed with His glory that is breathed upon you from heaven. In Jesus Name.

GIVE GOD YOUR ALL

Father, You have said, it is a time to rejuvenate our soul in the Lord.

Rejuvenation comes by prayer, Bible reading, seeking God for the destiny He has planned for your life, reaching out to others in kindness, witnessing about Jesus, living to please Him, loving your spouse, your children and family. Just give Jesus first place in your life and everything else will fall into place.

We will soon meet Him for His return draws closer and closer. All our works will follow us into heaven and we will be living throughout eternity with Jesus, even ruling and reigning with Him, as we live godly lives here on earth. Follow your heart when the Lord impresses you with what He wants you to do and what the Bible says to do. Then run from anything that leads you away from godliness and His will.

"I beseech you therefore, brethren, by the mercies of God, that ye present your bodies a living sacrifice, holy, acceptable unto God, which is your reasonable service.
And be not conformed to this world: but be ye transformed by the renewing of your mind, that you may prove what is that good, and acceptable, and perfect, will of God." Romans 12:1-2

Be tremendously blessed. May the presence of Jesus rest upon you and give you peace, a sound mind, and wisdom from above. In Jesus Name.

FACE OF JESUS

"For the righteous Lord loveth righteousness; and His countenance doth behold the upright." Psalm 11:7

The Lord's face is looking upon you with love and favor. When Jesus returns, we shall see Him face to face in all His glory.

One day while praying for a missionary in Tunis, Tunisia, the Lord appeared and when I looked into His eyes they were so full of indescribable compassion that I fell before Him weeping. Just the look in His eyes, the beautiful unbridled look of compassion in was something to behold.

"As for me, I will behold thy face in righteousness: I shall be satisfied, when I awake, with thy likeness." Psalm 17:15

"Behold, what manner of love the Father hath bestowed upon us, that we should be called the sons of God: therefore the world knoweth us not, because it knew Him not." I John 3:1

You cannot imagine the all-encompassing love and compassion in the most beautiful, indescribable eyes of Jesus looking down upon you right now. Are you wounded? He understands. He was wounded for your transgressions and carried them to the cross He died on. Are you afraid? He defeated that fear on the cross and exchanged it for faith – faith in Him. Are you discouraged, brokenhearted, lonely, gripped with sorrow, rejected in years gone by? Jesus felt all your pain in His body and carried it to the cross so you could be healed. His eyes are full of compassion for you. This is compassion that goes so deep and is so real that there are no words to express what was seen in His eyes.

"He is despised and rejected of men; a man of sorrows, and acquainted with grief: and we hid as it were our faces from Him; He was despised, and we esteemed Him not. Surely He hath borne our griefs, and carried our sorrows: yet we did esteem him stricken, smitten of God, and afflicted. But He was wounded for our transgressions, He was bruised for our iniquities: the chastisement of our peace was upon him; and with His stripes we are healed." Isaiah 53:3-5

And He is still being rejected by mankind. But one day we shall see Him in all His glory. Oh what a day that will be. Praise the glorious name of Jesus.

GOD IS SPEAKING

"Seeing ye have purified your souls in obeying the truth through the Spirit unto unfeigned love of the brethren, see that ye love one another with a pure heart fervently." I Peter 1:22

Father, may they know so well the voice that comes from the Lord. There are tremendous spiritual blessings - heaped up and running over - when you obey the Lord. He will usually speak to you through His Word or by His Holy Spirit to your heart. Note also that the Word and the Holy Spirit and the voice you hear will always agree. Obedience gives you spiritual understanding. Your relationship with the Lord grows. When He speaks, the response is to obey. Then your desires will begin to change and you no longer hold so tightly to that which pulls you away from the Lord. There will be new life come into your soul when you obey God. A new peace will settle into your spirit. You will read your Bible with deeper understanding. Obedience opens you to many wonderful blessings that are life-stabilizing.

May you be abundantly blessed. Declare with me, "Today the Lord is going to abundantly bless my life and will guide me in His perfect will." May God's protection be all around you and His grace, love and favor rest upon you.
In Jesus Name.

STAND STRONG

"For whatsoever is born of God overcometh the world: and this is the victory that overcometh the world, even our faith. Who is he that overcometh the world, but he that believeth that Jesus is the Son of God." I John 5:4-5

Lord, bless these precious ones. Because you are born of God, we pray you will make it a practice of doing right at all times and at all cost. May you stand up and be counted among the faithful who love the Lord and want to please Him with all your heart. May you practice avoiding that which might not be God's best. The Lord is your life.

"If ye then be risen with Christ, seek those things which are above, where Christ sitteth on the right hand of God. Set your affection on things above, not on things on the earth." Colossians 3:1-2

The purity of Christ dwells in your hearts. Christ in you is your hope of glory. May you be content to walk in love and holiness everyday. The Lord will shower you with His multiplied blessings and you have light and happiness in your heart. May you enjoy the wonderful blessings of His presence. The Lord is with you. He is standing beside you and will help you to stand strong. In Jesus Name.

WALKING WITH JESUS

There are qualities in you that God finds very wonderful because He put them there. Christ in you is never out of control. Your confidence is in God and He never is overwhelmed. His hands are weaving a character pattern that is becoming more and more beautiful in your life. Be at ease with the Lord who walks by your side.

There was a vision of Jesus taking the hand of this person like He was saying, "Come walk with Me." They looked straight ahead in perfect ease, without distraction, not looking down, nor to the right or left, and the Lord said, "Walk in lockstep with Me and at My pace." Then there was a whispered message that He is guiding and is walking with my hand in His toward a goal.

"Thou hast proved mine heart; thou hast visited me in the night; thou hast tried me, and shalt find nothing: I am purposed that my mouth shall not transgress." Psalm 17:3

"The just man walketh in his integrity: his children are blessed after him." Proverbs 20:7

May the sweet and lovely presence of the Lord settle down upon you and you find yourself in awe of Jesus Himself. He is speaking kindness and a peaceable spirit into your life. He looks upon you as a rare jewel that will one day fill His kingdom in heaven. His blessings on you are materializing every day showing you His deep and caring love. You are extremely blessed. In Jesus Name.

OPEN YOUR HEARTS

You are blessed by the Lord who loves you. He will open new doors of opportunity for you because you are going to see blessings that have never been seen before. As you yield your heart to Jesus you will have a richer and more glorious relationship with Him. May He send precious friends into your life. The Lord is taking all the not-so-good times and turning them into opportunities of ministry. Your light will shine brighter and brighter as you open your mouth and declare the Word of God to others. May you stand committed to the Lord and reap the blessings of Him living His life through you.

Some live life for the worldly thrills of today which lasts but for a moment, but we live life for eternity with the Lord which is unending. The world will either live with God or they will die without Him.

"Submit yourselves therefore to God. Resist the devil, and he will flee from you. Draw nigh to God, and He will draw nigh to you." James 4:7-8

Be blessed as you keep the line open in conversation with God. Stay on the line with Him and keep talking. He listens and never hangs up. You never know what might develop. You may hear the sweetest message ever. It will be an experience for sure. You will be blessed. In Jesus Name.

HIS LOVE FOR YOU

May the blessings of the Lord be upon you and His hand guide you forever. You be graced with a baptism of love and godliness. You shine like a star, because you walk with the Lord. As you pray, why not ask Him to reveal the deeper truth that is hidden in your Bible as you study to show yourself approved unto God. You will be surprised when you realize what Christ in you, your hope of glory, really means. The depth of that truth alone will make your spirit soar.

"He that dwells in the secret place of the Most High shall abide under the shadow of the Almighty:
I will say of the Lord, He is my refuge and my fortress: my God; in Him will I trust.
Surely He shall deliver thee from the snare of the fowler, and from the noisome pestilence.
He shall cover thee with His feathers and under His wings shalt thou trust: His truth shall be thy shield and buckler." Psalm 91:1-4

Be abundantly blessed. All heaven is behind you. You have support from every angle. God is right there with you. He never moves. He stands with you in every circumstance, in every situation, and nothing shall defeat you as you continuously lean on the Lord for guidance and help. God and you is a win/win relationship of the highest standard. He is an incredible person and to walk with him is an extraordinary experience. In Jesus Name.

HIS WORD BRINGS FREEDOM

"Then spake Jesus again unto them, saying, I AM the light of the world; he that followeth Me shall not walk in darkness, but shall have the light of life." John 8:12

"If ye continue in my Word, then are ye my disciples indeed: And you shall know the truth, and the truth shall make you free. If the Son therefore shall make you free, ye shall be free indeed." John 8:31, 32, 36

Sweet and wonderful blessings abide in your heart when you walk in the truth of God's Word and follow Jesus to live a life pleasing to your heavenly Father. He imparts to you those things which are a part of Him. You are constantly receiving deeper truth of who God really is. That sets you free.

When God speaks, the earth keeps silent. He is the last word on the subject. He is the alpha and the omega. His Word stands firm and unmovable. When He speaks everything is released, and the wheels are put into motion to fulfill every dot and tittle of what He says. There is no power on earth that can alter the truth of the Word of God. He works all things after the counsel of His own will.

May the blessings of the Lord bring freedom to your soul, mind, heart, body and spirit. Press into Him until you receive what is rightfully yours. In Jesus Name.

SHOW THE LORD KINDNESS

"Blessed be the God and Father of our Lord Jesus Christ, who hath blessed us with all spiritual blessings in heavenly places in Christ: According as He hath chosen us in Him before the foundation of the world, that we should be holy and without blame before Him in love." Ephesians 1:3-4

Father, move on their hearts to consider You.

It is good to show the Lord kindness and be thoughtful of Him. He is with you every day and very often we get busy and forget to give Him any attention. Simply ask Him to fill your heart with love for him. Loving Jesus will bring spiritual changes and He will reveal Himself to you in a brand new way. He wants us to pray without ceasing, always staying in contact with Him, talking to Him about everything. He is your constant companion. Honor him with your obedience.

May you be drawn to the sweet and loving nature of the Lord and be refreshed by His presence. Everything you need is in the Lord. In Him you have one hundred percent multiplied with unlimited zeros behind it. In Him you lack nothing.

May the Lord give you the wonderful blessings of wisdom and knowledge and revelation in the knowledge of Him. In Jesus Name.

DRAW NEAR TO GOD

Father, show these Your heart. The sweet blessing that the Lord gives every day is to keep focusing on Him. His sweet presence over you as born-again washed-in-the-blood children of God is to keep you protected and loved. He knows what is going on in the world and He is in total control. Our focus is on the Lord and that keeps our minds in peace. Lord, You are the King of Kings and the Lord of Lords. There is no power greater than You. We give You honor and praise. In Jesus Name.

"Open to me the gates of righteousness: I will go into them, and I will praise the Lord: this gate of the Lord, into which the righteous shall enter. I will praise thee: for thou hast heard me, and art become my salvation." Psalm 118:19-21

May you begin to pray with a new anointing. It is prayer that gets God involved, that defeats all the enemy's plans. It defeats him personally. Prayer is insistence upon God's will being done. It puts you in touch with Jesus. May his blessings overflow your life. Reach up and touch the hem of His garment and receive healing to the depths of your soul and walk refreshed and strengthened with new blessings. In Jesus Name.

JESUS' RESURRECTION DESTINY

Jesus' resurrection destiny is to bring many sons into His glory.

"And now, O Lord God, thou art that God, and thy words be true, and thou hast promised this goodness unto thy servant: Therefore now let it please thee to bless the house of thy servant, that it may continue forever before thee: for thou, O Lord God, hast spoken it: and with thy blessing let the house of thy servant be blessed forever."
II Samuel 7:28-29

The Lord walks beside you to bless you and your house. The language of the Lord is entirely different than the language of the world. God says you are blessed exceeding abundantly above all that you could ever ask or think. The world is dominated by Lucifer and will say anything that limits God.

"And be not conformed to this world: but be ye transformed by the renewing of your mind, that ye may prove what is that good, acceptable, and perfect will of God." Romans 12:2

Believe God. Believe Him for the above-and-beyond, the over-the-top, the miraculous. Think big. You have a big God who speaks big blessings over you. There is nothing impossible with Him. Have faith in God. God has adopted you as His sons and daughters. You are an heir of God.

"But when the fullness of the time was come, God sent forth His Son, born of a woman, made under the law, to redeem them that were under the law, that we might receive the adoption of sons. And because ye are sons, God hath sent forth the Spirit of His Son into your hearts crying, Abba Father. Wherefore thou art no more a servant, but a son; and if a son, then an heir of God through Christ."
Galatians 4:4-7

You and your house are blessed as you yield up to God everything you have. God will work and He will bless. In Jesus Name.

WISE CHOICES

The coming of the Lord draws near when we shall be caught up in the air to meet Jesus.

"But this one thing I do, forgetting those things which are behind, and reaching forth to those things which are before, I press toward the mark for the prize of the high calling of God in Christ Jesus.

"For our conversation is in heaven; from whence also we look for the Savior, the Lord Jesus Christ; Who shall change our vile body that it may be fashioned like unto His glorious body, according to the working whereby He is able even to subdue all things unto Himself." Philippians 3:13, 14, 20, 21

May the Lord reveal to your hearts the importance of pressing toward the mark for the prize of the high calling of God in Jesus, so that all your choices be pleasing to Him and you build up your godly inheritance which will be given you when you stand before the Lord and give an account of your life. Every single day you commit your life to God He conforms you to be Christ-like here on earth and, in eternity your reward will be great.

May the sweet and precious blessings of the Lord be upon you as He opens up the meaning of faith in the Word of God to believe Him for miracles. In Jesus Name.

GREATER THINGS FROM GOD

We speak the blessing of the Lord over your life today. We declare and decree that you will be lifted to new heights and deeper depths in God. The center of all life is God, Jesus and the Holy Spirit. That is where it all began. May the Lord wrap His loving arms around all of you and breathe resurrection life deep into your souls. May He give you a wonderful refreshing of the blessings of goodness into your spirit and revive your heart. Reach up and take hold of the hand of the Lord that is extended to you

"For thou hast made him most blessed forever: thou hast made him exceeding glad with thy countenance." Psalm 21:6

There is nothing you need that He will not give you. His presence is moving across the land to give His double portion anointing and blessing to those who will follow Jesus. Walking with Him is the greatest most incredible blessing you will ever experience in this life and in the life to come.

"Great deliverance giveth He to His king; and showeth mercy to His anointed, to David, and to His seed forevermore." Psalm 18:50

In Jesus Name.

GOD REIGNS

Secure your future by following Jesus. To overcome the enemy, submit to the Lord. Carnality destroys the desire to obey the Lord and stops your moving forward in God. May you choose to walk with the Lord by being faithful to read your Bible and pray and willing to put God first.

"Behold, I give unto you power to tread on serpents and scorpions, and over all the power of the enemy: and nothing shall by any means hurt you." Luke 10:19

"And it shall come to pass afterward, that I will pour out My Spirit upon all flesh; and your sons and your daughters shall prophesy, your old men shall dream dreams, your young men shall see visions:
"And also upon the servants and upon the handmaids in those days will I pour out My Spirit." Joel 2:28, 29

The blessings of these mighty signs in the last days will awaken many hearts to serve the Lord with white hot fervency. When the Lord pours out His Holy Spirit there will be signs following. Awaken from any sleepiness or disinterest and take your stand at the station that God has ordained you to fill. Many miracles will soon become normal occurrences, for the day will require it. In Jesus Name.

HOLINESS OBTAINED IN CHRIST

"I am crucified with Christ; nevertheless I live, yet not I, but Christ liveth in me: and the life which I now live in the flesh I love by the faith of the Son of God, who loved me, and gave Himself for me." Galatians 2:20

"For me to live is Christ." Philippians 1:21

"But be filled with the Spirit." Ephesians 5:18

"There is no fear in love; but perfect love casteth out fear." I John 4:18

"Love not the world, neither the things that are in the world. If any man love the world, the love of the Father is not in him. For all that is in the world, the lust of the flesh, and the lust of the eyes, and the pride of life, is not of the Father but is of the world. And the world passeth away, and the lust thereof: but he that doeth the will of God abideth forever." I John 2:15-17

"But if we walk in the light, as Jesus is in the light, we have fellowship one with the another, and the blood of Jesus Christ His Son cleanseth us from all sin." I John 1:7

"But the Lord shall be unto thee an everlasting light, and thy God thy glory. Thy sun shall no more go down, neither shall thy moon withdraw itself; for the Lord shall be thine everlasting light, and the days of thy mourning shall be ended." Isaiah 60:19, 20

May God's blessings rest upon you and completely restore everything back to you that has been stolen or lost. God is in the restoration business of bringing you back to Him with fuller blessings, greater love, and the Holy Spirit doing mighty works through you. May you hunger and thirst for righteousness. In Jesus Name.

WHO ARE YOU V. WHAT YOU DO

May the Lord bless you to rise up and be counted among those who follow Jesus and obey His word. May you fall in love with Him. He is coming back for us very soon and we want to be watching and waiting for Him with great expectancy. All comfort and blessings are in Him. It is the Lord who folds His arms around you and blesses you with safety. He is all-powerful. He is full of love for you. Nothing satisfies your soul like the person of Jesus. Searching for things and desiring stuff to satisfy only ends up leaving an unsatisfied feeling. You never reach the place where enough is enough. But when you pray and read your Bible and desire to know who Jesus is and listen to what He says, then a sweet satisfaction comes over you and the things of this world loses its drawing power.

In the Bible in Acts chapter 8, in the account of an Ethiopian eunuch, he had been to the right place, Jerusalem. He had been for the right purpose, to worship. He was reading the right book of Isaiah, the scripture, but he was returning home unsatisfied. God sent Philip to preach Jesus to him that day and the eunuch was saved and he went home satisfied in his soul, because he had found the Person of Jesus as his Savior. The emphasis is transferred from the place to a Person.

"My soul, wait thou only upon God, for my expectation is from Him. He only is my rock and my salvation; He is my defense; I shall not be moved. In God is my salvation and my glory; the rock of my strength, and my refuge is in God. Trust in Him at all times; ye people, pour out your heart before Him; God is a refuge for us." Psalm 62:5-8

May you be blessed in miraculous ways. In Jesus Name.

APPOINTED FOR BLESSINGS

The Lord has given you blessings beyond number. He has equipped you with Christ who is in you. He has given you the Holy Spirit to guide you into all truth. Jesus is praying for you twenty-four hours, seven days a week as He sits at the right hand of God. God is your Father, your protector. Everything you need comes from Him. You are blessed because you are forever connected to the holy, righteous and pure powers in heaven. The Lord has called you to be blessed with holy and honorable living.

You are marvelously blessed:

"By pureness, by knowledge, by longsuffering,, by kindness, by the Holy Spirit, by love unfeigned, By the Word of truth, by the power of God, by the armor of righteousness on the right hand and on the left." II Corinthians 6:6-7

May you be workers together with Him, yielded and obedient to His voice. Inside you are hidden gifts that need to come forth and be used to be a blessing to others. You are a treasure, like a precious jewel, that the Lord is fashioning for today's needs. Take the blinders off that hide God's greatest blessings that are already given to you. It is all your choice. May you choose life, abundant life, that will reap a harvest of eternal blessings laid up for you in heaven. In Jesus Name.

OBEY WHEN GOD CALLS

May you be blessed by giving attention to the thoughts going through your mind. The more positive your thoughts, the more positive and blessed your life will be. Every word of your vocabulary is important. Ask God to fill your mind with a vocabulary that He is pleased with. It is even good to spurn every ungodly amusement, including television, if it robs you of God's blessings, so that your life is patterned after Jesus and you reap what He has provided.

"Abstain from all appearance of evil." I Thessalonians 5:22

"Whereunto He called you by our gospel, to the obtaining of the glory of our Lord Jesus Christ." II Thessalonians 2:14

God desires that you walk with the glory of Jesus shining all over you, because you are saved by His blood and you have new life in Him. Refuse to let the enemy of your soul rob you of God's best. The trade-off is wasted goods. If you are not enjoying God's peace and joy in your heart, then the enemy has robbed you of what is yours. God's peace and joy are gifts and blessings for you to enjoy. Decide to make a strong determination that no power will take away what is rightfully yours. Everything you need is lying on the table ready for you to pick up and fly with the eagles, liberated, set free from shackles, and soak in the ever-loving goodness of God. It is yours. Accept it.

"And in thy majesty ride prosperously, because of truth and meekness and righteousness; and thy right hand shall teach thee wonderful things." Psalm 45:4

"But in the living God, who giveth us richly all things to enjoy; That they do good, that they be rich in good works, ready to distribute, willing to communicate; Laying up in store for themselves a good foundation against the time to come, that they may lay hold on eternal life." I Timothy 6:17-19

In Jesus Name.

CHRIST-CENTERED LIFE

The Lord is rich in His mercy toward you. He is a powerful merciful God. In Him you have been protected from the harsh affects of hard trials because He has encapsulated you with His hand. You are brought forth refined and have been made into a glorious chosen vessel for the Master's use. You shine with His glory. Your life reflects who Jesus is. Jesus is the one who provides for everything whatever may be needed for soul and body. In the measure that you put your trust in Him, in that measure will His supply be given to you.

"The God of Israel is He that giveth strength and power unto His people. Blessed be God." Psalm 68:35

"Thou art fairer than the children of men: grace is poured into thy lips: therefore God has blessed thee forever." Psalm 45:2

Be abundantly blessed in all your right choices. In Jesus Name.

OBEDIENCE OBTAINS YOUR GOAL

There is tremendous blessing in obeying the Lord with complete joy of heart.

The Lord is blessed when He sees someone loving Him enough to be obedient to Him. We are to simply obey and leave all the consequences with Him.

The Apostle Paul was always unconscious of himself, because he was recklessly abandoned to the call, and was totally separated by God for one purpose - to proclaim the Gospel of Christ.

"Neither yield ye your members as instruments of unrighteousness unto sin; but yield yourselves unto God, as those that are alive from the dead, and your members as instruments of righteousness unto God." Romans 6:13-14

"For as many as are led by the Spirit of God, they are the sons of God.
The Spirit itself bears witness with our spirit, that we are the children of God." Romans 8:14, 16

Precious Lord, for those who are children of the living God, we ask that you lead them in the way that you want them to take, living with your abounding grace and love all around them, and making them into the likeness of Jesus Himself.

And for those who need to accept Jesus as their personal Savior, it is written in Romans 10:9-10:

"That if thou shalt confess with thy mouth the Lord Jesus, and shalt believe in thine heart that God hath raised Him from the dead, thou shalt be saved. For with the heart man believeth unto righteousness, and with the mouth confession is made unto salvation."

Believe this scripture in your heart, and confess that you have just accepted Jesus as your Savior, and you are now a child of God, born into the body of Christ. In Jesus Name.

GOD'S UNLIMITED LOVE

"Sow to yourselves in righteousness, reap in mercy, break up your fallow ground; for it is time to seek the Lord, till He come and rain righteousness upon you." Hosea 10:12

May God bless you with a heart and soul of purity, godliness, holiness and righteousness.

May He bless you in ways that you will become more like Jesus.

May your eyes and ears and mouth be protected from all evil and you overflow with the goodness of Jesus.

May you be blessed by a holy encounter from the Lord, where He moves upon your spirit and joy fills your heart with wondrous happiness.

May your heart be soft and tender toward the Lord and you hear His sweet voice as He talks to you.

May He bless you with great favor and intelligence.

Shine, precious ones, shine for Jesus. He is so worthy of your love and devotion. In Jesus Name.

QUALIFIED VERSUS QUALIFIES

The blessing of the Lord is upon you to restore you and to remove all reproach off you. He is come to inspire you for you are designed for greater things than you have the ability to see. His gifting in you and His power and anointing on you will perfect you and will cause you to come to the higher place that He has prepared for you. Lay aside oppression and come to Him and He will fill you with great joy, for His kingdom is a kingdom of joy. In the Spirit of the living Lord, there is joy, liberty, peace and power. The anointing will be poured out upon you so that you will not only be restored, but you will be strengthened beyond what you have ever known. These are the days of His glory coming on His people to impact the world.

"And I will restore to you the years that the locust hath eaten, the cankerworm, and the caterpillar, and the palmerworm, my great army which I sent among you. And ye shall eat in plenty, and be satisfied, and praise the name of the Lord your God that hath dealt wondrously with you, and my people shall never be ashamed." Joel 2:25-26

You will never find a trace of harshness in the Lord. His ways of dealing with you are always tender and loving and with great concern. His heart is humble and if you saw Him, you would say He has such a meekness and gentleness about Him. It would be so profound and so different from any character trait you have ever seen in people that you would be in awe at His presence. Jesus has no character flaws. He has taken on the likeness of God the Father and glorious awesomeness of the Holy Spirit. It will be wonderful – beyond comprehension – to spend eternity with them in heaven.

This is your blessing. This is what makes it all worthwhile. In Jesus Name.

EQUIPPED FOR GOD'S USE

The Lord is calling forth blessings upon a people who will walk in integrity and rise up a standard of righteousness, and stand by it. Blessings are upon those who are willing to stand against all that undermines truth, faith, and spiritual complacency. They will become a great and powerful army of mighty spiritual warriors who will be anointed by the Spirit of God to take down the enemy where they find him. They will affect a great and resounding victory that will bring honor to the Lord Jesus Christ.

"Being filled with the fruits of righteousness, which are by Jesus Christ, unto the glory and praise of God." Philippians 1:11

"And they that know thy name will put their trust in thee; for thou, Lord, hast not forsaken them that seek thee." Psalm 9:10

May you stand fully clothed with the spiritual armor God has provided, and His wonderful blessings will be upon you night and day. In Jesus Name.

MOVE IN FAITH

Sometimes we allow certain things to come into our lives that later causes trouble. So "close the gate" to that thing and have nothing else to do with it. It prevents the blessings from getting through to you.

"Where no wood is, there the fire goeth out." Proverbs 26:20.

So as wood is to keeping a fire going, so does ungodly associations, wrong choices and bad habits keep a continual fire and disruption going in the life of a Child of God. Follow the Lord and let nothing rob you of His blessings.

"The legs of the lame are not equal." Proverbs 26:7

Neither is the godly who walk with the ungodly.

"The wisdom of the prudent is to understand his way." Proverbs 14:8

God will give you wisdom and understanding to know what is good in His eyes. Whatever brings you peace, follow it.

"There is a way which seemeth right unto a man: but the end thereof are the ways of death." Proverbs 14:12

This is deception. So believe God in faith to keep your eyes open and your mind and thoughts clear. Stay close to the Lord. Read your Bible and mentally get under His wings and you will be protected.

May the Lord guide you to always seek the way that sheds the light of God on your pathways, for in this your vision will always be clear and your mind rests in peace. May you be blessed with God's best. In Jesus Name.

WILLING SUBMISSION

The wonderful blessing of purposing in your heart early in the day to stand committed to God in all your actions and words gives you such joy and peace of mind. May the Lord bless you to possess an attitude of willing submission to be directed by God's will.

The Lord bless you with a desire to live a life of purity, righteousness, holiness and godliness whereby you will live the most incredible life possible. May there be no desire in your heart to dabble here and there in sin or waste your hours and days on worldly interests that would rob you of God's best.

Father, draw all these closer to your heart. May they continually grow spiritually in their walk with You. May they pray to make godly choices so You can bless them in their right decisions. In Jesus Name.

"For thou, Lord, wilt bless the righteous; with favor wilt thou compass him as with a shield." Psalm 5:12

"Verily, verily, I say unto you, He that believeth on Me, the works that I do shall he do also: and greater works than these shall he do; because I go unto My Father." John 14:12

May the Lord do great exploits in your life and when He uses you, be careful to always give Him the glory. The great blessings come when your eyes are always on the Lord and not on yourself or someone else. Seek the way of humility and study to be so. May you be blessed in wonderful ways and with life-changing results. In Jesus Name.

CONNECTED TO JESUS

If you could see with spiritual eyes, you would see yourself connected to Jesus. His presence from the throne room in heaven fills your heart and mind and body and soul and spirit. He is enhancing your abilities to make you more skilled. That which has hindered you will drop off and be taken away. Hindrances make you weak as water, but they are taken away by the Lord. The marvelous works that He has created you for will come forth. Nothing has passed you by. You have not missed His perfect will. The character that he has been developing in you has made you stronger and you will soon be more conscious of the Lord's presence. He never removes His hands from your life. You never have to go it alone because the Lord has been there all the time. The root of your existence is the Lord. He is your solid core.

"Preserve me, O God: for in thee do I put my trust." Psalm 16:1

God is concerned for the oppressed and will lift them up, restoring what has been taken from them.

May you be blessed with faithfulness and steadfast obedience to God which marks the life of faith. Faith is a whole new way of life. Be blessed to daily depend upon God, walking with Him moment by moment. Faith says that God alone is enough. In Jesus Name.

GO HIGHER

May the God of heaven be with you every step of the way.
May He bless you with a greater presence of His Spirit.
May you seek to get closer to the Lord, letting Him have His way, always yielding and obeying Him.
May you believe God with a strong faith for the impossible.
May He direct your circumstances to bring the greatest blessings.

Prayer is the greatest work. Prayer opens more doors, eliminates more problems, and lives in the realm of the impossible. Prayer takes you into the presence of the Lord.

"In all things showing thyself a pattern of good works: in doctrine showing uncorruptness, gravity, sincerity, sound speech, that cannot be condemned; that he that is of a contrary part may be ashamed, having no evil thing to say of you." Titus 2:7-8

May your words and actions be appropriate for every situation, filled with wisdom, always desiring to please the Lord. May the wonderful, abounding blessings of the Lord be upon you and His presence guide you wherever you go. In Jesus Name.

PRAISE HONORS GOD

It is good to praise and give thanks, according to the commandment of David the man of God. May the Lord bless you by filling your heart with gladness, both with thanksgivings, and with singing songs of praise unto God for He is wonderful and marvelous. There is continual praise around the throne of God. And He dwells in and inhabits the praises of His people. When you praise the Lord, His presence comes upon you and fills the atmosphere around you. There are millions of things for which you can praise God. Praise lifts burdens. Praise lifts up the name of the Lord and honors Him.

"But thou art holy, O thou that inhabitest the praises of Israel." Psalm 22:3

"For God had made them rejoice with great joy. For in the days of David and Asaph of old there were chief of the singers, and songs of praise and thanksgiving unto God." Nehemiah 12:43, 46

In Nehemiah's day, they praised and gave thanks unto the Lord and singers were brought into Jerusalem. We do not know their names. They were just called "singers" and they sang loud, so that the joy of Jerusalem was heard even afar off. They praised the Lord with musical instruments of David the man of God. The priests' sons praised with trumpets. The Levites praised with cymbals, psalteries, cornets which were curved horns, and with harps.

"Rejoice in the Lord, O ye righteous: for praise is comely for the upright. Praise the Lord with harp; sing unto Him with the psaltery and an instrument of ten strings. Sing unto Him a new song; play skillfully with a loud noise." Psalm 33:1-3

Be gloriously blessed as you lift up the holy name of Jesus. In His Name.

JESUS IS WITH YOU

The love of God draws you away from all that is not keeping with God's holiness. May you live every day so that there may come to you an abundant reward that is laid up for you in heaven. Jesus is with you, Jesus is before you, Jesus is behind you, Jesus is in you, Jesus is beneath you, Jesus is above you, Jesus is on your right, Jesus is on your left, Jesus is with you when you lie down, Jesus is with you when you sit down, Jesus is with you when you arise.

"Humble yourselves therefore under the mighty hand of God, that He may exalt you in due time." I Peter 5:6

"And the fruit of righteousness is sown in peace of them that make peace." James 3:18

Every time you yield to the Lord, you unlock the gates for Him to come in and walk beside you. "C'mon Lord, walk with me through this day and guide me every step of the way. Help me to show love to everyone I meet and reach out to those who need someone who cares. I ask that You enable me to accomplish all You have given me to do so that this evening, You and I can reflect upon the day and You will help me keep my life always open to Your will." Then follows the blessing. In Jesus Name.

YIELD TO JESUS

"This is the day which the Lord hath made; we will rejoice and be glad in it." Psalm 118:24

May the Lord speak into your day and fill your heart with praise and expectancy for all He has spoken over you.

What you do today will be part of the history that is being recorded in heaven for which deeds you will give an account. Your deeds will be gold, silver and precious stones versus hay, wood, and stubble. To sit before the Lord in quietness and ask Him to speak what is on His heart for you will set you on the right course and will enrich your life. Excellence will be imparted. New talents are given. God will open your eyes to see the great things He has planned for you. Simply obey Him.

"For other foundation can no man lay than that is laid, which is Jesus Christ.
"Now if any man build upon this foundation gold, silver, precious stones, wood, hay, stubble;
"Every man's work shall be made manifest: for the day shall declare it, because it shall be revealed by fire; and the fire shall try every man's work of what sort it is.
"If any man's work abide which he hath built thereupon, he shall receive a reward.
"If any man's work shall be burned, he shall suffer loss: but he himself shall be saved; yet so as by fire." I Corinthians 3:11-15

The Lord bless you on the earth as He will in heaven. May all your works, deeds, words and thoughts be worthy of an eternal reward in heaven. We declare "no loss" over your life. In Jesus Name.

BELIEVE GOD'S WORD

And to all you precious ones:

"Blessed of the Lord be his land for the precious things of heaven, for the dew, and for the deep that coucheth beneath, and for the precious fruits brought forth by the sun, and for the precious things put forth by the moon, and for the chief things of the ancient mountains, and for the precious things of the lasting hills, and for the precious things of the earth and fullness thereof, and for the good will of him that dwelt in the bush, let the blessing come upon the head of Joseph." Deuteronomy 33:13-16

May the blessings of Joseph be your portion. The Lord will cause everything He has made to be a blessing to you. He will pull blessings from the abundance that He has created to give you. Believe the Lord. Have faith in God. He will do exceeding and abundantly more than you ever expected.

"Praise ye the Lord. Praise, O ye servants of the Lord, praise the name of the Lord. Blessed be the name of the Lord from this time forth and forevermore. From the rising of the sun unto the going down of the same the Lord's name is to be praised." Psalm 113:1-3

In Jesus Name.

ULTIMATE PERFECTION

May you be sensitive to the leading of the Holy Spirit, for you are entering a time when you can truly put an end to procrastination and tie up loose ends. The Lord is surrounding you with an extraordinary measure of favor and grace to do all that is necessary. As soon as you choose to be done with the things that have overwhelmed you, the burden of heaviness will lift and you will be free to move forward. The Lord will enhance and accelerate your every effort but you must take the first step.

"Wherefore, my beloved brethren, let every man be swift to hear; slow to speak; slow to wrath; For the wrath of man worketh not the righteousness of God.
"Wherefore lay apart all filthiness and superfluity of naughtiness, and receive with meekness the engrafted word; which is able to save your souls.
"But be doers of the word, and not hearers only, deceiving your own selves." James 1:19-22

"Now the God of Peace, Make you perfect in every good work to do His will, working in you that which is well-pleasing in His sight, through Jesus Christ, to whom be glory forever and ever. Amen." Hebrews 13:20-21

May Jesus dwell in you richly calling you into a life dedicated to His perfect will. Jesus in you has given you wisdom, and righteousness, and sanctification, and redemption. Christ in you is your hope of glory. The grace of the Lord Jesus, and the love of God, and the communion of the Holy Spirit be with you.
In Jesus Name.

LOVE JESUS

There is a depth in God that few people ever experience and yet it is there for all who will hunger and thirst for righteousness. When you desire something from the Lord long enough, He will always give it to you, and especially if it will be used for His glory. It is worth everything to pay the price. And to have the Lord walking close to you every day and night is the greatest blessing you could ask for. God has created a natural covering of protection over each of your lives saving you for a great awakening where you will be brought into the destiny He has planned for you. From His perspective you are His children, dressed in robes of righteousness.

"I will greatly rejoice in the Lord, my soul shall be joyful in my God; for He hath clothed me with garments of salvation, He hath covered me with the robe of righteousness, as a bridegroom decketh himself with ornaments, and as a bride adorneth herself with her jewels." Isaiah 61:10

"Thou shalt also be a crown of glory in the hand of the Lord, and a royal diadem in the hand of thy God." Isaiah 62:3

What a thrilling promise God has spoken. You are seen as royalty in the eyes of the Lord. You are raised up to be bright lights that shine in a dark world. It is Christ in you that will always prevail and lift you up for His glory. Truly you are the blessed people of God. In Jesus Name.

GOD IS WONDERFUL

The Lord is so inspiring. He awakens continuously great gifts that He has invested in you from His throne room. His is a mighty God. The life He leads you into is all-bountiful and superabundant. He • leads you to enjoy many of the joys of life today that you never were aware of yesterday. Each day is a gift from the Lord. Every morning He reaches out His hand and offers you a rare jewel of experiences that will expand your borders and lift you to new heights from His glorious creation into which you have been born. He offers to walk with you and talk with you so you can experience the wonder surrounding Him. He freely offers you all that He has - and all that He is. You serve a mighty God.

"That men may know that thou, whose name alone is Jehovah, art the Most High over all the earth." Psalm 83:18

"My soul longeth, yea, even fainteth for the courts of the Lord: my heart and my flesh crieth out for the living God.

"Blessed are they that dwell in thy house: they will be still praising thee.

"For the Lord God is a sun and shield: the Lord will give grace and glory: no good thing will He withhold from them that walk uprightly.

"O Lord of hosts, blessed is the man that trusteth in thee." Psalm 84:2, 4, 11, 12

May these scriptures speak deep into your soul and awaken a hunger and thirst for more of God. You are greatly blessed of your God. His hand is upon you. He will guide you into all truth and the truth shall set you free.
In Jesus Name.

MINISTRY OF THE UNNOTICED

The Lord is interested in the small things. Many times He takes the small things and multiplies them into mountains of blessings. He took seven loaves of bread and a few little fishes and fed four thousand men, beside women and children, and He took up of the broken meat that was left seven baskets full. Matthew 15: 34-38

The Lord is interested in blessing the smallest things that you give to Him. He will show you what they are.

Small bits are put in the mouths of horses and we turn about their whole body.
Ships which are so great are turned about with a very small helm by the helmsman. Likewise, the tongue is a little member that boasts great things but is a fire that defiles the whole body.

Out of the same mouth proceed blessing and cursing. Does a fountain send forth at the same place sweet water and bitter or salt water and fresh water?

The Lord asks that you give to Him the smallest things that bring mixture into your life, because they stand in the way of obtaining what God has for you. Allow the Holy Spirit to reveal to your heart what is robbing you of God's best.

"And they were not able to resist the wisdom and the spirit by which He spake." Acts 6:10

Be abundantly blessed as you live a life dedicated to the Lord. Jesus believes in you. In Jesus Name.

CHOOSE THE LIFE THAT LIVES

The Lord's hand is reaching out to draw you to Him and bless you. He desires a closer relationship with you. His will is to refresh your spirit. Your walk with Him is of utmost importance. Keep your Bible close by. Just pick it up and read a scripture or two. The Word is powerful. You will gain insight and strength and be blessed moment by moment every day. You will find the Word speaking about the very thing you are experiencing. The Lord is always with you to bless you.

In these days your decisions will take on greater significance, and your choices will be as seeds sown that will produce a harvest of greater magnitude than you have previously ever experienced. It is, therefore, to your advantage to choose according to the Lord's wisdom. It is vital that you draw near to Him, that you walk in truth and humility, and that you exercise the utmost integrity in all that you think, say, and do. May you ask for wisdom, and be wise.

"Through wisdom is a house builded; and by understanding it is established; and by knowledge shall the chambers be filled with all precious and pleasant riches. A wise man is strong, yea, a man of knowledge increaseth strength." Proverbs 24:3-5

May Jesus reach down and bless you sweetly and abundantly. He enjoys loving you. In Jesus Name.

WORD OF GOD

"For the Word of God is quick, and powerful, and sharper than any two-edged sword, piercing even to the dividing asunder of soul and spirit, and of the joints and marrow, and is a discerner of the thoughts and intents of the heart." Hebrews 4:12

We are talking about your Bible, holding within its pages the most powerful words ever written by man, telling a story from Adam to the end of time, words that are living and creative, that goes into your heart and creates faith and calls you to believe in Jesus as your Savior and redeemer so you will spend eternity with Him in heaven. Nothing but the Word of God can transform your life and give you wisdom, joy, wholeness, healing, deliverance, and instruction on how to walk with the Lord and live a life well-pleasing to Him. By reading your Bible you understand who God is. There is no other book in the world like your Bible and the words contained therein. No generation has ever been able to destroy it for it is God who protects it for all the world to read.

The Bible is written with elaborate goal-directed planning. That every dot and tittle agrees with one another from beginning to end is nothing short of the mastermind of Almighty God. Let us take note of the first verse, "In the beginning God created the heavens and the earth." Studies show that the enumeration of sevens being accidental is only one in 678,623,072,849. This elaborate design of sevens runs through the words of the first verse of the Bible.

May you be abundantly blessed as you read God's Word and be strengthened with might by His Spirit in your inner man and be rooted and grounded in God's love. In Jesus Name.

LOVE HEALS

May a blanket of God's love cover you. His love heals. His love reaches to the depth of your soul and straightens out all the entanglements that have robbed you of His best. The love of the Lord is refreshing to your spirit. It is a fact that Jesus simply loves you completely.

"Be filled with the fruits of righteousness, which are by Jesus Christ, unto the glory and praise of God." Philippians 1:11

"That you would walk worthy of God, who hath called you unto His kingdom and glory." I Thessalonians 2:12

"And there is hope in thine end, saith the Lord, that thy children shall come again to their own border." Jeremiah 31:17

May the blessings of peace, contentment and joy be upon you. May the burdens on your heart be lifted and all of them are cast on the Lord for He cares for you. Be blessed with contentment for He holds you in His hands. In Jesus Name.

GOD IS GOD

The Lord has laid up in heaven an inheritance for you. There are temporal and spiritual blessings every day and they are all spoken by the Lord in your Bible. May there be a longing in your soul to forever receive the overflow blessing of an opened heaven. Seek Jesus. May your heart long to know Him. He is the great blessing. May you learn from Him. As you pray, may He show you His glory, the glory of the only begotten Son of God. This earth will pass away but all you can gain in knowledge and understanding of the holy Jesus who gave Himself on a cross for your salvation is the holy Lord that walks and talks with you every day.

Know you not that you are the temple of God, and that the Spirit of God dwells in you?

"Grace be to you and peace from God the Father, and from our Lord Jesus Christ. Who gave Himself for our sins, that He might deliver us from this present evil world, according to the will of God and our Father. To whom be glory forever and ever. Amen." Galatians 1:3-5

The Lord's hand of mercy and grace and love and healing is upon you and you are blessed. In Jesus Name.

YOU AND JESUS ARE ONE

"But we see Jesus, who was made a little lower than the angels for the suffering of death, crowned with glory and honor; that He by the grace of God should taste death for every man." Hebrews 2:9

It is wonderful to honor Jesus and esteem Him to the highest degree. He gave His life with dignity for your salvation that through death He destroyed him that had the power of death, that is, the devil. He is touched when you give him honor with every thought of Him. He gave everything He had so you could have eternal life in heaven with Him. He is powerful. And He sits at the right hand of almighty God making intercession for you without ceasing. So take heed, brethren, lest there be in any of you an evil heart of unbelief, in departing from or forsaking the living God. Rather, honor Him first and foremost.

"Wherefore in all things it behooved Him to be made like unto His brethren, that He might be a merciful and faithful high priest in things pertaining to God, to make reconciliation for the sins of the people. For in that He Himself hath suffered being tempted, He is able also to succor them that are tempted." Hebrews 2:17-18

May you be blessed with a clear mind, having understanding of God and His plans and purposes for your life. He desires you to lay aside anything that would cause you to depart from Him. You are blessed with a love for righteousness and are anointed with the oil of gladness. In Jesus Name.

JESUS NEVER FAILS

"Wherefore seeing we also are compassed about with so great a cloud of witnesses, let us lay aside every weight, and the sin which doth so easily beset us, and let us run with patience the race that is set before us. Looking unto Jesus the author and finisher of our faith; who for the joy that was set before Him endured the cross, despising the shame, and is set down at the right hand of the throne of God." Hebrews 12:1-2

You have an encouragement - a great cloud of witnesses. You have an encouragement also to lay aside every weight, and the sin which does so easily beset you. You are also encouraged to run with patience the race of winning Jesus as the Bridegroom of your soul. The Lord wants you to be marked off from the rest of the world and be recognized as the children of God. The Light of Christ shining through you will draw others to want to know Him as Savior.

May you be blessed and made complete in every good work to do God's will, working in you that which is well-pleasing in His sight, through Jesus Christ.
In His Name.

JESUS THE POTTER

"By Him therefore let us offer the sacrifice of praise to God continually, that is, the fruit of our lips giving thanks to His name." Hebrews 13:15

"In everything give thanks: for this is the will of God in Christ Jesus concerning you." I Thessalonians 5:18

When things go well, it is easy to thank the Lord for everything that happens. It is "kinda'" easy to thank the Lord when things are not quite that great. But it is another thing to thank the Lord in everything. The "everythings" mean the good, the bad and the ugly. How often are we called to thank God for all things - all the time. This takes faith and grace. It means you must look at everything from God's standpoint, not yours. It takes trusting Him. It takes putting it all in His hands.

"And we know that all things work together for good to them that love God, to them who are the called according to His purpose." Romans 8:28

Believe that the blessings of His goodness and kindness are revealed to you and will give you peace. Allow the blessings of God's hand carrying you through life be realized as one of your greatest blessings. May His sweet grace rest upon you. In Jesus Name.

LEARN TO DO GOOD

All the wonderful benefits that we have as believers came at an enormous cost to God. He gave His only Son to be crucified on a rugged cross and put all the wicked sins of the world from Adam to the sins of the last person to be born, upon Jesus who became sin for us, though He was spotless, never committed any sin, and was totally holy. Our sins are forgiven only by the sacrificial death of Jesus and by His blood that came from His hands and feet and side when they nailed Him to His cross. Forgiveness of sin did not come easy. God could not forgive sin because He is a holy God who cannot look upon sin. It took Jesus on the cross to give us forgiveness.

And by Jesus dying on the cross, satan was totally defeated, stripped of all power he once had and is destined to a lake of fire world without end. When God raised Jesus from the dead, He rose in total triumphant victory over death, hell and the grave. The only way sin and satan exists today is by deception and lies. He is the father of lies. But he is totally defeated by Jesus.

"Submit yourselves therefore to God. Resist the devil, and he will flee from you. Draw nigh to God, and He will draw nigh to you." James 4:7-8

"Come now, let us reason together, saith the Lord; though your sins be as scarlet, they shall be as white as snow; though they be red like crimson, they shall be as wool." Isaiah 1:18

May you receive His miraculous blessing of repentance and forgiveness, thanking God for His incredible gift of living your life apart from the evil works of the world. In Jesus Name.

OBEDIENCE LEADS TO LIFE

Obedience to the Word of God is a matter of choice. The Lord never forces you to be obedient to follow what He has said is His plan for your life. You cannot improve on what God says you ought to do. His way gives life and peace and an over-the top relationship with Him. There is so much contentment when you obey the Lord.

The key to obedience is, "If any man will come after Me, let him deny himself, and take up his cross daily, and follow Me." Luke 9:23

Taking up your cross daily is an act that simply says you do not love someone else more than Him – not even "yourself." Doing what pleases yourself more than what pleases God is always putting what you want to do before obedience to the Lord. But when we obey the Lord, thousands are blessed because God moves through your obedience to other lives and multiplies the blessing of your obedience.

"Seeing ye have purified your souls in obeying the truth through the Spirit unto unfeigned genuine love of the brethren, see that ye love one another with a pure heart fervently." I Peter 1:22

May you receive the blessing of being obedient to God. Simply honor the Lord from your heart, which brings abundant blessings. In Jesus Name.

ASCENDING TOWARD GOD

There is a world of joyous experiences awaiting you today and every day until the Lord returns. There is a fountain of grace from past generations that has been passed down to you. Every prayer that was ever prayed from days gone by is waiting before the Lord to be answered and be a blessing to you.

"And the very God of peace sanctify you wholly: and I pray God your whole spirit and soul and body be preserved blameless unto the coming of our Lord Jesus Christ. "Faithful is He that calleth you who also will do it." I Thessalonians 5:23-24

May God bless you in the highest possible way and draw you into His plan for your life. Receive His blessings that cover you with an awe of His presence. Expect a miracle that has been passed down to you from past generations.
In Jesus Name.

MERCIFUL AND GRACIOUS

"And the Lord passed by before him, and proclaimed, The Lord, The Lord God, merciful and gracious, long-suffering, and abundant in goodness and truth, Keeping mercy for thousands, forgiving iniquity and transgression and sin." Exodus 34:6-7

"And He said, My presence shall go with thee, and I will give thee rest." Exodus 33:14

When the Lord says His presence shall go with you, He means just that. Believe when the Lord says something. Have no doubt. The Lord's presence is not only with you but His presence goes before you and prepares a path that will give you rest and peace. When you walk with the Lord, all hell has to flee. All He does is walk and nothing in heaven or hell can resist Him or stand in His way. He is the Lord. He is Jesus. The authority He carries is of God who made heaven and earth. You carry that same authority when His presence goes with you.

May you stand tall, with your shoulders square, and look the enemy in the face and say, "Be gone. I belong to Jesus and you cannot touch my life."

God and man will be as one in the action of service against the enemy. So be gloriously blessed with happiness of heart, joy in your spirit, favor that exceeds your highest expectation, and fulfillment of all the promises God has spoken over your life. In Jesus Name.

GOD IS HOLY LOVE

May the Lord reveal to your heart what tremendous significance the cross of Christ has and how it daily impacts your life. When God sent His Son to die on the cross so that you might have forgiveness of sin, He established you forever in His love. Once you accept Jesus as your personal Savior, God launched you into a realm where Jesus dwells and gave you what is needed to live a victorious life. There are two realms, the heavenly and the earthly. He gave you the knowledge to know the difference. He also provided prayer so that you can come into His presence to join Him in a holy relationship; a Bible to read for spiritual strength; faith to believe God will do what He promised in the Bible; and love that impels you to forever walk with the Lord. In God's provision, you are always established, secure, confident, sound in mind, body, soul, spirit, and heart, considerate, loving, unwavering in your walk with the Lord, and everything you need. He cannot fail you, ever.

Because God gave His Son so that you will live eternally with Him, this places a value on your life that few truly comprehend. He paid the ultimate price for you to live above the earthly realm that opposes Jesus and His tremendous sacrifice. The earthly realm is where the anti-Christ spirits live. This is out of your realm. You live in the eternal-life-realm where you continuously see God in action. Miracles become daily occurrences. This is where blessings flow.

"For whatsoever is born of God overcometh the world; and this is the victory that overcometh the world, even our faith." I John 5:4

You are gloriously blessed and so beautiful in the sight of the Lord. In Jesus Name.

PURPOSE OF LIFE

The purpose of life is to win Christ as the Bridegroom of your soul. It is He who empowers and enables you to overcome anything and everything that comes from satan. You are victorious over all temptation and all troublesome matters, because it is the Lord who comes in and wipes the slate clean when you call upon Him. He is daily preparing you to rule and reign with Christ in heaven. You are destined for greatness here on earth so that you can be blessed with all spiritual blessings in heavenly places in Christ. Jesus endured the cross and God set Him at His own right hand in the heavenly places.

"And hath raised us up together and made us sit together in heavenly places in Christ Jesus. That in the ages to come He might show the exceeding riches of His grace in His kindness toward us through Christ Jesus." Ephesians 2:6-7

This is talking about you. This is speaking of what God has planned for you in heaven. So while you live and move and have your being, live wholeheartedly for Christ so that you might win Him as the Bridegroom of your soul.

Be abundantly blessed. The Lord shows forth His loving kindness toward you each and every day. In Jesus Name.

GOD'S PERFECT TIMING

May the Lord bless you and establish His Word toward you and draw your heart ever closer to Him. May you come into the Lord's favor in every area of your life.

"Thou shalt arise, and have mercy upon Zion; for the time to favor her, yea, the set time is come." Psalm 102:13

God's timing for many of His greatest manifestations and work for you is now. The waiting has ended. The time has now come for all that you have prayed for, desired and hoped for will now come to pass. All your dreams which seemed to have been forgotten have only caused God's anointing to increase greater upon them year by year. There is no 'rejecting' because God is now 'injecting' them with resurrection power. All of your life, God has been preparing you for today. The time has come that He is bringing you out and is imparting in you new visions, divine projects, new creations, new gifts that have been buried inside you. God is putting resurrection power into all that He has put within you.

"You shall also be a crown of glory in the hand of the Lord, and a royal diadem in the hand of thy God." Isaiah 62:3

May faith arise in your heart to believe God for the impossible. All His blessings that He has promised you will surely come to pass. He will restore back to you all that was taken from you. In Jesus Name.

JESUS IS CALLING

The Lord is tenderly calling you to come to the cross, lay down all your burdens there, give all your cares to Jesus and lean on Him to guide you through to victory. There is a glorious side in your walk with the Lord. When you realize that He is your constant companion and you can call on Him anytime, you gain strength spiritually and you can truly say He was there all the time. The rush of life will always pull you away from taking time with the Lord. There won't be time to pray, read your Bible, or even go to church. Apathy can set in and the things of God become unimportant.

"If ye love me, keep My commandments. And I will pray the Father, and He shall give you another Comforter, that He may abide with you forever; even the Spirit of truth; whom the world cannot receive, because it seeth Him not, neither knoweth Him; but ye know Him; for He dwelleth with you, and shall be in you. I will not leave you comfortless: I will come to you." John 14:15-18

Father, we speak blessing over my precious family and pray You do a quick work in their lives. We ask that You give them a heart that is yielded to You. May they make You their first consideration. When other things are put first, there is confusion. Jesus, show them Your love. Bless them mightily with all spiritual blessings. In Jesus Name.

GOD SEEKS YOU

Father, we pray that every person in my family will hear the voice of the Lord and establish an ongoing relationship with You. Give them a heart of flesh, a truly tender heart toward You. May their emotions be uncrushed by circumstances of the past or present. Whomever you touch is immediately changed. Their mind is clear and their choices are directed by the Holy Spirit. They delight in obeying Your will. Lead them in a way of righteousness and give them wisdom to walk with understanding. Strengthen them spiritually. Visit them in the night seasons and guide them in the daytime. Draw them ever closer to You. In Jesus Name.

"How much better is it to get wisdom than gold! and to get understanding rather to be chosen than silver." Proverbs 16:16

"Know ye not that ye are the temple of God, and that the Spirit of God dwells in you?" I Corinthians 3:16

Give these precious ones wisdom and understanding to hear the deep truths of Your Word and accept with great grace the multiple blessings that come through the Spirit of God that dwells in them. Bless these with Your holiness and kindness and tender mercy, O Lord. In Jesus Name.

LOVE OF GOD

There is much blessing when you hold onto the love of God. It steadies you. It makes you feel connected. You are not alone and forsaken. The love of God gives you strength to carry on and not give up.

At the root of God's love is His ultimate sacrifice when He gave His only begotten Son to die on the cross for your salvation. When you see that complete sacrifice, you have no doubt that He loves you. His love is unconditional. He died for the most wretched, wicked piece of humanity to the nice, worldly, dressed-up sinner on earth. He loved the world and died that the souls of mankind be made clean by His blood.

"That if thou shalt confess with thy mouth the Lord Jesus, and shalt believe in thine heart that God hath raised Him from the dead, thou shalt be saved. For with the heart man believeth unto righteousness; and with the mouth confession is made unto salvation." Romans 10:9-10

May you be blessed by the love of God deep within your soul. The more you know Him, the more you know His love. Be abundantly blessed by His love.
In Jesus Name.

GOD'S PURPOSES

May you keep in touch with Jesus so you will have an open ear to hear His voice. May you delight to do His will. It is His highest plan for your life. God's Word must be allowed to discipline your judgment as to His will. If His Word is absorbed, there will come a better judgment of God's thoughts toward you. Lord, bless them to be yielded to walk in a higher will that brings them closer to God.

"For God, who commanded the light to shine out of darkness, hath shined in our hearts, to give the light of the knowledge of the glory of God in the face of Jesus Christ. But we have this treasure in earthen vessels, that the excellency of the power may be of God, and not of us." II Corinthians 4:6

You are a new creature in Christ, old things are passed away, and behold all things are become new. May you grow in the grace and knowledge of Jesus and become wholly His. In Jesus Name.

DO IT HEARTILY TO GOD

"And whatsoever ye do, do it heartily as to the Lord, and not unto men: Knowing that of the Lord ye shall receive the reward of the inheritance: for ye serve the Lord Christ. But he that doeth wrong shall receive for the wrong which he hath done: and there is no respect of persons." Colossians 3:23-25

It is good to seek those things which are above, where Christ sits on the right hand of God. Set your affection on things above, not on things on the earth. There is a choice here; you can choose to follow Jesus or seek earthly things which draw you away from the Lord. He asks that you put off all these: anger, wrath, malice, blasphemy, filthy communication out of your mouth. Lie not one to another, seeing that you have put off the old man with his deeds when you accepted Christ as your Savior. But now put on the new man Jesus. Lord, may they yield to you and put on therefore, as the elect of God, a heart of mercy, kindness, humbleness of mind, meekness, long-suffering; forbearing one another, and forgiving one another, if any man have a quarrel against any, even as Christ forgave you, so also forgive him.

The true and holy blessings of the Lord Jesus Christ are yours with all tenderness and peace. In Jesus Name.

BLESSINGS

The Lord is here to minister to your every need. He is your constant companion, your faithful High Priest, who makes intercession for you according to the will of God. Lord, we ask that everything work for their good every day of every year. Block out the enemy that nothing evil touch their lives. Draw them into Your presence. May they be daily conformed to the image of Christ. Remove all that hinders their walk with the Lord. Strengthen them in their inner man and enable them to walk in truth, for this is pleasing to You.

"That ye would walk worthy of God, who hath called you unto His kingdom and glory. For this cause also thank we God without ceasing, because, when ye received the Word of God which ye heard of us, ye received it not as the word of men, but as it is in truth, the Word of God, which effectually worketh also in you that believe." I Thessalonians 2:12-13

May the Lord bless you with health and happiness, favor and intelligence, wisdom and knowledge. Bless them abundantly. In Jesus Name.

WALK WITH THE LORD

May the Lord bless you beyond measure. May you walk in lock-step with the Lord as He guides you to go deeper and come up higher in God. The Lord has taken your hand in His and is walking with you. All He asks of you is to look up and walk at His pace. When you do, He will move out all obstacles that have been in your way, and you will move with ease, because the Lord is holding your hand. You are fully under His guidance. You are shielded by Him. Nothing can touch you to pull you off course, because your hand is in His. You are gloriously blessed by His matchless love. His confidence becomes your confidence.

"Thou wilt show me the path of life: in thy presence is fullness of joy; at thy right hand there are pleasures forevermore." Psalm 16:11

God is so real. Find great comfort and peace in His matchless love. Be abundantly blessed. In Jesus Name.

YOU ARE BLESSED

May the Lord raise you up on wings of eagles. May you soar upon the wind of the Holy Spirit and view things from high and lofty places that are above this earth. May you come to Jesus and be renewed in strength, come and be healed and refreshed. May the Lord bring encouragement to your heart. So come with faith to receive that which the Lord is doing. May the Holy Spirit move you into the fullness of His purpose. So come and be healed, refreshed and renewed. He is waiting for you to ask. His blessings are there.

May you be accepted in the sight of all people and always behave yourself wisely, the Lord giving you extraordinary wisdom and integrity. It is God who wants to expand your borders to be a greater blessing to those around you. Walk confidently and securely with Jesus who enables you. May you receive love from all those who know you.

"And David behaved himself wisely in all his ways; and the Lord was with him." I Samuel 18:14

Bless you abundantly as God keeps you safe and protected. In Jesus Name.

SMALL THINGS SPEAK LOUDLY

It is a beautiful sight to look into the eyes of the one who truly loves the Lord. Somehow the kindness of Jesus comes through. They have a look of sincerity. You feel they are trustworthy. They are very easy to communicate with. There is a warmth about them. All these and more are characteristics that reflect Jesus in your eyes.

There are other things about your face that people see.

Your mouth: "The mouth of a righteous man is a well of life." Proverbs 10:11
Your mouth: "The mouth of the just brings forth wisdom." v. 31
Your love: "Love covers all sins." v. 12
Your lips: "In the lips of him that has understanding wisdom is found." v. 13
Your lips: "The lips of the righteous know what is acceptable." v. 32
Your tongue: "The tongue of the just is as choice silver." v. 20
Your words: "In the abundance of words transgression does not cease." v. 19

The Lord says,

"Blessed is the man that heareth Me, watching daily at My gates, waiting at the posts of My doors. For whoso findeth Me findeth life, and shall obtain favor of the Lord." Proverbs 8:34-35

May the Lord form habits in you that will develop a strong character. May you be surrounded with great love and happiness . In Jesus Name.

LOVE WAS CREATED TO CREATE

"And be not conformed to this world, but be ye transformed by the renewing of your mind, that ye may prove what is that good, and acceptable, and perfect, will of God." Romans 12:2

"If it be possible, as much as lieth in you, live peaceably with all men." Romans 12:18

"Be not overcome of evil, but overcome evil with good." Romans 12:21

Father, pour out Your ultimate blessing of love into the minds, hearts, souls, bodies and spirits of all my family. May Your love cover their minds to think good thoughts. May Your love sink deep into their hearts to speak words of love, for out of the heart the mouth speaks. May the blessing of Your love fill them to overflow with confidence and assurance. May they feel Your all-consuming love. May Your love reach into every crevice of their lives and heal them. Restore them to newness of life. Bless them with the eyes of the Holy Spirit to see clearly and to think clearly. May the awe of feeling God's love and wisdom inspire them. They are Your children, created in the image of God. Hold them tightly to Your chest at all times, Lord. In Jesus Name.

PRAYER IS POWERFUL

"But He said, Yea rather, blessed are they that hear the Word of God, and keep it." Luke 11:28

"But be ye doers of the word, and not hearers only, deceiving your own selves." James 1:22

Let each one be found faithful to pray. Whatever happens to you at any time, when you pray about it and talk to the Lord until you feel He has answered, all the stress and strain goes and a sweet assurance fills your heart. Prayer brings you into the presence of the throne of God where Jesus sits at the right hand of God. Prayer draws the Lord into your circumstances. Prayer moves the hand of God.

There was a woman in London who began praying that Dwight L. Moody would come from America to London and preach in her church. The months went by and a year and over but still she prayed. Nobody knew of it but herself and God. No change seemed to come but still she prayed. And that is the touchstone of true prayer. And the Spirit of God moved that man of God across the ocean and into London, and into their church. Do you not believe that some day when we stand before the Lord that we shall find that the largest single factor in that ten days' work, and in the changing of tens of thousands of lives under Moody's leadership is that woman in her effectual prayers. Yet no one knows her name.

"Pray without ceasing.
"In everything give thanks: for this is the will of God in Christ Jesus concerning you. "Quench not the Spirit.
"Abstain from all appearance of evil.
"And the very God of peace sanctify you wholly, and I pray God your whole spirit and soul and body be preserved blameless unto the coming of our Lord Jesus Christ. "Faithful is he that called you, who also will do it." I Thessalonians 5:17-19, 22-24

May the wonderful blessings of the Lord be upon you and grace and peace from God. In Jesus Name.

FAITH GIVES CONFIDENCE

May the sweet presence of Jesus move upon your heart, mind, soul, spirit and body and give you heavenly peace. All the bustle of life, the clamor for your time, the hurrying here and there, settles down when you reach up and take hold of the hands of Jesus. He will carry you through. He will lift you up. He will bless you because He is personally watching over your life. He protects you and loves you. It is Jesus who is the same yesterday, and today, and forever. He holds you in the hollow of His hand. You are precious to Him. You have great value. He died for you to live an overcoming life. He made a world and put you in it and trusts you to take care of His business. He trusts you to make a better world by letting your light shine for Him. You are glorious to Him. You were created by the hands of Jesus. And you are beautiful in His sight.

"Now faith is the substance of things hoped for, the evidence of things not seen." Hebrews 11:1

"Now the God of peace, that brought again from the dead our Lord Jesus, that great shepherd of the sheep, through the blood of the everlasting covenant." Hebrews 13:20

A man from Nigeria was telling the story about people in Mozambique seeing the dead raised, the blind see, and the lame walk. Miracles are happening all the time because the people have this simple faith that believes God will do it. There's no clutter in their lives. They have nothing. But they believe God is a God of miracles. Nothing is impossible with God and because of their faith, it happens. Praise the Lord.

You are abundantly blessed. You are set apart unto God and He will bless you because you are identified as His blessed children. In Jesus Name.

MANIFOLD WISDOM OF GOD

"Jesus stood and cried saying, If any man thirst, let him come unto Me, and drink. He that believeth on me, as the scripture has said, out of his belly shall flow rivers of living water." John 7:37-38

As in life, so is it true spiritually, that when you become thirsty, nothing satisfies your thirst like water. No other beverage will quench your thirst. So it is spiritually. Jesus says, "If anyone is thirsty, let him keep coming to Me and drinking." Nothing satisfies your spiritual thirst like Jesus Himself. Whosoever puts his trust in Jesus, as the Scripture says, rivers of living water will flow from his inmost being. The Holy Spirit from within you flows out to others. Your words are life-giving.

You are a messenger of the Lord sent to your world with the message of Jesus. You are sent to be a blessing to others. Jesus says, "I AM the light of the world: he that follows me shall not walk in darkness, but shall have the light of life." Your words are blessed with a powerful affect on others. Just like God sent Jesus into the world to speak His Word, so now Jesus has you in the world to speak His Word to others.

"And ye shall know the truth, and the truth shall make you free." John 8:32

Be wonderfully blessed as the Lord leads you in His truth, the eyes of your understanding being enlightened, that you may know the fullness of who Jesus really is. In Jesus Name.

VALUABLE TO GOD

May the effectual working of Jesus' mighty power flow through you as you understand the unsearchable riches of Christ. May you reach your full potential that He has created within you so that you may attain to the high calling of God. You are pure gold in His eyes and are of inestimable value.

There is a quality of richness in life that God wants to bless you with. Reach up and claim it. It is there for you to take from His outstretched hand. You are brought near to Jesus through the shedding of His blood. The Cross freed you from this evil world, without hope and without God. The ways and habits of the world are useless to you. You are now of God's making, created in union with Jesus for a life of good actions already prepared by God for you to do. So imitate God, as His children, and live a life of love.

"That in the ages to come He might show the exceeding riches of His grace in His kindness toward us through Christ Jesus." Ephesians 2:7

May you be blessed with the kindness and love of the Lord. Be blessed by His great deliverance through mercy, so that by grace you might come to be considered righteous and become heirs of eternal life.

May there be a moral decision about sin, so that no tears of regret are shed from not having pressed through to attain God's best for you. In Jesus Name.

FAITH IS TOTAL TRUST

"Faith cometh by hearing and hearing by the Word of God." Romans 10:17

"Without faith it is impossible to please the Lord." Hebrews 11:6

"For we walk by faith, not by sight." II Corinthians 5:7

"Now the just shall live by faith." Hebrews 10:38

"Faith without works is dead." James 2:20

"Whatsoever is not of faith is sin." Romans 14:23

"I live by faith of the Son of God." Galatians 2:20

"The just shall live by his faith." Habakkuk 2:4

"The just shall live by faith." Romans 1:17

"For therein is the righteousness of God revealed from **faith to faith**." Romans 1:17

"We all are changed into the same image from **glory to glory**." II Corinthians 3:18

You receive long-living faith by hearing and reading the Word of God. As you soak in God's Word, the blessings come as the righteousness of God is revealed to you. Doubt will lift off you as your faith in the righteous God increases. Then you will enter into liberty and freedom where the Spirit of the Lord is. But we all, with open face beholding as in a glass the glory of the Lord, are changed into the same image from glory to glory, even as by the Spirit of the Lord.

The Spirit gives life, even abundant life, transforming life, radiant life, overcoming life. Your appearance changes. The grief, the turmoil, the look of anxiety leaves your face and you have a brand new look. Christ is becoming more real and He is filling up all the hollow places inside you with His glorious presence. And you are changed into the same image of Christ from glory to glory.

May you be blessed with a new-found, new-created confidence and assurance and self-awareness that will give you more happiness than you can imagine. You are truly the blessed of the Lord. In Jesus Name.

ENTIRE RELIANCE ON GOD

We do not create our own destinies, we are simply privileged to discover and fulfill them. God has an assignment for you that only you can fulfill. This is why you were born. God wants to bring you into the very center of what He has called you to do. May you let God be first, family second, friends third and the world fourth. May your life be a divine example of the goodness of God. May you be Holy Spirit anointed to be the best you can be as a strong Christian loving the Lord with all your heart, as a husband or wife, as a mother or father, as a friend, and as a Good Samaritan to the world.

"And whatsoever ye do in word or deed, do all in the name of the Lord Jesus, giving thanks to God and the Father by Him." Colossians 3:17

"I thank my God, making mention of thee always in my prayers, "Hearing of thy love and faith, which thou hast toward the Lord Jesus, and toward all saints; That the communication of thy faith may become effectual by the acknowledging of every good thing which is in you in Christ Jesus." Philemon 1:4-6

May the wonderful blessings of Jesus rest upon you and bring you into perfect contact with the purposes of God. In Jesus Name.

TO BE LIKE JESUS

"Wherefore also we pray always for you, that our God would count you worthy of this calling, and fulfill all the good pleasure of His goodness, and the work of faith with power: that the name of our Lord Jesus Christ may be glorified in you, and ye in Him, according to the grace of our God and the Lord Jesus Christ." II Thessalonians 1:11-12

May the Lord bless you with hope, assurance, righteousness and favor. May the changeless brightness of His glory shine into the very depths of your soul and life. May you wear the glory of the Lord. You are altogether lovely to the Lord. He sees you as a rare jewel, His blessed creation. His banner over you is love. May He shower you with love where you are blessed forevermore. May He pull out all that would block your way and speak on your behalf so all creation hear His voice and see the blessings that are on you.

"Not by might, nor by power, but by My Spirit, saith the Lord of Hosts." Zechariah 4:6

May the holiness of God surround your life and give you peace and favor.
In Jesus Name.

PRAYER

Lord, place Your hand upon all these precious ones and guide them in the ways of righteousness. Combat all the forces of evil that may war against them and raise them up in victory over their enemies. Lighten their load that they cast all their cares upon Jesus who cares for them. May they be among those in the Bride of Christ who overcome and will rule and reign in heaven with Jesus. May their lives be fruitful and be used of God to influence many people to believe in Jesus as their personal Savior.

Walk with them every day, precious Lord, and speak peace to their hearts. May they look into Your face and receive that undisturbed peace. May they never allow anything to hide Your face from them but always be in right standing with You. You are faithful and will establish them. In Jesus Name.

"Now the God of hope fill you with all joy and peace in believing, that ye may abound in hope, through the power of the Holy Spirit." Romans 15:13

The Lord bless you and keep you and cause His face to shine upon you. The blessings of Jesus are upon you. In Jesus Name.

PURE IN HEART

Hezekiah, king of Israel, "trusted in the Lord God of Israel so that after him was none like him among all the kings of Judah, nor any that were before him. For he clave to the Lord, and departed not from following Him, but kept His commandments, which the Lord commanded Moses. And the Lord was with him, and he prospered whithersoever he went forth." II Kings 18:5-7

Blessings will always follow when you put your focused trust in the Lord. He sees your trust, He hears your prayers, and He will never fail you. His strength will keep you strong. Glory in His holy name; let the heart of them rejoice that seek the Lord. Seek the Lord and His strength, seek His face continually.

May there be godly blessings on your life that are especially given you that will flood your soul with peace and confidence. He is a God of comfort. May He bless you with assurance and stability.

"O give thanks unto the Lord; for He is good; for His mercy endures forever." I Chronicles 16:34

In Jesus Name.

WALK IN NEWNESS OF LIFE

"Grace and peace be multiplied unto you through the knowledge of God, and of Jesus our Lord According as His divine power hath given unto us all things that pertain unto life and godliness, through the knowledge of Him that hath called us to glory and virtue."
II Peter 1:2-3

Look at these wonderful blessings. Everything that God is, becomes yours in the Lord Jesus Christ. As you submit to His will He will work through you what He wants. May you allow His nature to be imparted into you as you become more Christ-like everyday. The more you yield your life to the goodness of Jesus, the more you become like Him.

It is wonderful to be with the person who lets Jesus live through them in gentleness, kindness, love, thoughtfulness, and good works. God is rich in mercy and grace toward you. All His precious promises are yours.

May your heart be open to the Lord so He can pour His rich abundance into your life. May you comprehend that God's majesty and grace and power are to be manifested in you. God is able to make all grace and glory and virtue abound in you. May His nature be your nature as His blessings come through you to other people.

"Whereby are given unto you exceeding great and precious promises; that by these you might be partakers of the divine nature, having escaped the corruption that is in the world through lust."
II Peter 1:4

May the blessings of the Lord be showered upon you in abundance as you spend more time reading your Bible to understand what God and the world is all about. In Jesus Name.

REJOICE IN GOD

The windows of heaven are open over you, and the blessings are being poured out. We make declaration that everything in you is blessed. God's healing power is working in your life and every part of your body, mind, soul, spirit and heart is made whole for "By the stripes of Jesus, you are healed."

The Lord wants His people well. He wants you blessed with a joyful and happy attitude. May His resurrection life raise you up to live victoriously over all the cares of life. God has shielded you with His grace. May you believe His precious promises by faith and enter into a whole new realm of standing on the Word of God in faith.

You are exalted above all these cares. You are established by faith that God is presently working all things out for you. Why? He loves you with an unconditional love that follows you wherever you may go. He never leaves you. He never forsakes you. At the end of every day, you will realize that the Lord was with you every step of the way. There is a mighty God guiding you. You will never lose your way. He has been there all the time.

"Let them shout for joy, and be glad, that favor my righteous cause: yea, let them say continually, Let the Lord be magnified, which hath pleasure in the prosperity of His servant. And my tongue shall speak of thy righteousness and of thy praise all the day long." Psalm 35:27-28

May you be blessed with a new awakening of who Jesus really is and learn His ways in order to understand His heart. In Jesus Name.

SPIRITUAL GARMENTS

"I will greatly rejoice in the Lord; my soul shall be joyful in my God; for He hath clothed me with the garments of salvation; He hath covered me with the robe of righteousness, as a bridegroom decketh himself with ornaments, and as a bride adorneth herself with her jewels." Isaiah 61:10

In the eyes of the Lord, you are most precious to Him. He looks upon you as His costly jewels. He shows you His deep love by spiritually dressing you with garments of salvation, liberty, deliverance, prosperity, safety. He has covered you with a robe of righteousness, as a groom is adorned and as a bride wears her jewels. To Him, You are the blessed people of God. As a king is dressed in royal apparel because of his status as king, so the Lord has dressed you in holy apparel denoting your kinship to Jesus, the King of kings and Lord of lords. So the Lord God will cause righteousness and praise to spring forth in you. This is how He sees you when He looks at you from heaven. In Jesus Name.

TATUM'S SALVATION

Sometimes God surprises you with a "WOW" day. He goes above and beyond anything you had expected. It is at those times you realize just how close the Lord is in all your circumstances. While talking to Tatum on the phone this morning, the conversation led to my asking her if she had ever accepted Jesus into her heart. She said, "No." After gently explaining the plan of salvation to her, she asked Jesus to come into her heart and was saved. The time was 10:20 a.m., May 25, 2010. It was precious. So tender and so much love sweetly flowed into her little heart. This was indeed a "WOW" morning.

May the Lord give you a "WOW" day also. His love crosses all boundaries, goes into the deepest places, accepts and redeems all His precious ones from harm, raises you to the highest level, loves you from heaven to earth and then some, looks upon your hearts with all its cares and speaks gently into your spirit, "Peace be still." He calms every storm, reverses all hateful words spoken against you, throws up a barrier to block off and stop with a protective barricade against attacks, He reaches out and draws you toward Him out of the way of even verbal assaults and says, "You are accepted in the beloved Christ, and you are precious to Me."

"Praise be to the Father of our Lord Jesus, who has blessed us with all spiritual blessings in heavenly places in Christ. According as He has chosen us in Him before the foundation of the world, that we should be holy and without blame before Him in love." Ephesians 1:3-4

You are gloriously blessed. He is always reaching out to you with every need you have in His hands. In Jesus Name.

PRAY CONTINUALLY

"But we will give ourselves continually to prayer, and to the ministry of the Word." Acts 6:4

The strength that prayer and reading the Bible gives you is powerful. Every day we need food for our bodies to stay strong and healthy. So it is with the spiritual. We need to stay connected to the Lord by praying and reading the Word to show us how to live an overcoming life that is pleasing to the Lord.

May your choices be guided by the Holy Spirit so that you are always choosing that which brings life and makes you strong spiritually. You are God's masterpiece, a child of the Most High. You are one of a kind. You are wonderfully made by the Lord. He never made you inferior. You are destined for greatness. He sees you as the beautiful person He made. You were formed with the loving hands of a holy God.

"No weapon that is formed against thee shall prosper; and every tongue that shall rise against thee in judgment thou shalt condemn. This is the heritage of the servants of the Lord, and their righteousness is of me, saith the Lord." Isaiah 54:17

Negative words spoken against you, negative labels put upon you, negative judgments made against you, saying "you are" this or that, God says you are to cast them down as lies. That is not who you are. Rather, you are a winner. You are redeemed by the blood of Jesus and you are priceless. Your value to God and the world goes over the top. You are abundantly blessed and God loves you and He is for you. In Jesus Name.

TALENTS AND ABILITIES

Pursue your dream. Use your God-given talents that come so natural to you. Almost everything you purchase is the fulfillment of someone's dream. The stores and businesses are the fulfillment of someone's God-given ability. The buildings represent someone's architectural talents. Every container in your cabinet is the product of someone stepping out and pursuing their dream to develop that product. Through Edison's God-given talent, we have electricity and light bulbs and candles are now used primarily for decorative purposes. But because of the greatness and world-changing effect that Edison's invention would have on the world, God chose a man who had tenacity and sticktuitiveness that would not give up until it worked and after 10,000 attempts he succeeded. Grandma Moses painted her first picture when she was 85 and only painted for five years before she died, but today her paintings are worth hundreds of thousands of dollars. Ford built a motor and now we have cars. Louis Pasteur, the chemist and bacteriologist, developed Penicillin. Greatness was given to all God's creation to be a blessing to each other. What you do will bless and affect others.

God created you with greatness. My mother always wanted to paint, but never did; however, her talent to play the piano was wonderful and we had years of enjoyment listening to her play. My daddy had a God-given talent to play golf and shot a score of 67 when he was 67 years old. He could have been a pro golfer but he didn't have the money to pursue that dream. He would play 54 holes of golf almost every Sunday. Now his talent has been passed down genetically to all the men in our family. Everyone are great golfers and some of the women also. All the men and several women and children, both boys and girls have also inherited His natural talent to play ball.

Phillip, Kevin and Nathaniel inherited his ability to be fast runners. They are very talented, very fast.

"Blessed be the Lord, who daily loadeth us with benefits, even the God of our salvation." Psalm 68:19

You are blessed of the Lord, precious family. God is going to open the doors of opportunity and He will anoint you with the Holy Spirit to fulfill your destiny. In Jesus Name.

GOD IS GREATER

"For thus saith the Lord God, the Holy One of Israel; In returning and rest shall ye be saved; in quietness and in confidence shall be your strength." Isaiah 30:15

The Lord is with you in a greater way than He has ever been, for His hand is upon you for blessing. The light is shining brighter and brighter over your life. The Lord is leading you in His righteousness and is making your way straight. Think of the thing most difficult to deal with. Lay it in the lap of the Lord in prayer. Now trust Him with it. Believe in your heart that God is faithful and will answer your prayer. Your heart will be filled with joy because the Lord stands ready to defend your cause and will not let your enemies rule over you.

For the Lord will bless the righteous, and with favor will He surround you as with a shield. He will make a way where there is no way. He is gentle and tender toward you and calls you to walk worthy of Him. Are there any voids in your life? Is there any area where you are dissatisfied? Are your choices not bringing the results you intended? Then pray. The answer to all your questions is in Him.

Prayer, real prayer, getting in touch with God, having that secret touch with Him pulls it all together and you are able to see clearly. He will move heaven and earth for you. Trust Him. Have faith. Prayer is insistence upon God's will being done and opposes the will of the evil one.

"And whatsoever ye shall ask in My name, that will I do, that the Father may be glorified in the Son. If ye shall ask anything in My name, I will do it." John 14:13, 14

Be wonderfully blessed and raised to new life in Christ. In Jesus Name.

GRACIOUS WORDS

God created the world, and the heavens that relate to our world. He created man and woman, and everything on earth in just six days, and put the world in the hands of those who would serve Him as God over all. This is totally above and beyond what our minds can conceive. There is no limitation or boundary with God. He can do anything you need Him to do. Nothing is impossible with Him. When you read in the Bible all the manifold miracles He did for His people, you see how great and mighty is your God - and you are His child. Everything He has is yours. Look at all He created for you to enjoy. This is totally amazing.

"Stand up and bless the Lord your God forever and ever; and blessed be thy glorious name, which is exalted above all blessing and praise." Nehemiah 9:5

May you seek Him who is all merciful and gracious, so you can tap into His godly wisdom and be able to apply that wisdom in all you do. May the Spirit of the Lord be upon you and give you great faith to believe Him for the impossible and live an overcoming life of victory and abundant joy. In Jesus Name.

LOVE IS FOREVER

"Ye have not chosen me, but I have chosen you, and ordained you, that ye should go and bring forth fruit, and that your fruit should remain: that whatsoever ye shall ask of the Father in My name, He may give it you. These things I command you, that you love one another." John 15:16-17

May you be rooted and grounded in love, letting love be the underlying character and motive of all that you do. Love always ministers life and comfort. When you feel loved there is a solid sense of security. When you give love, you are at peace in your soul. Jesus is love. Love is the Spirit of God. Showing love to your family puts your family on a sound foundation and reaps good rewards for your future. What a loss not to give love to a child. The ultimate goal in life is to look like Jesus so that others may see Him through you. You are made in the image of God. Enjoy the ultimate blessing that is yours. Let nothing rob you of this blessing.

"As for me, I will behold thy face in righteousness. I shall be satisfied, when I awake, with God's likeness." Psalm 17:15

May the Lord bring many blessings into your life in ways you never thought possible. May the great and mighty hand of the Lord be always upon you.

In Jesus Name.

SEIZE YOUR MOMENTS

May you walk in the way of greater blessing by walking in love, with a mentality of selflessness, giving, nurturing, excelling in your dedication to Jesus, seeking to yield and obey His direction, and living above reproach. May you make a decision to get the mind of the Lord regarding building a sure foundation for today so that your future will become brighter and brighter. Because there is a law of God that we reap what we sow, may your sowing for today be such that will work toward a more solid and prosperous future. May you give today to the Lord to guide you upward toward a happier and freer tomorrow. The habits and thoughts of yesterday may need to be forgotten and forgiven so you can receive a much improved change and emotional healing. May the windows of heaven open and rain down multiplied blessings upon you with great favor and love.

"And they sang together by course in praising and giving thanks unto the Lord; because He is good, for His mercy endureth forever toward Israel. And all the people shouted with a great shout, when they praised the Lord, because the foundation of the house of the Lord was laid." Ezra 3:11

Oh that your hearts will be blessed and much encouraged and inspired with hope by the Holy Spirit. Lord, fill their hearts with Jesus, that they have dreams and visions of just how much You love them. In Jesus Name.

GOD IS IN YOUR TODAYS

God sees you in your perfected state and walking in your God-called destiny. The greatest blessings come when you seek first the kingdom and glory of God.

"The Lord thy God in the midst of thee is mighty; He will save, He will rejoice over thee with joy; He will rest in His love, He will joy over thee with singing." Zephaniah 3:17

The Lord has a sincere desire for your highest interests, both spiritual and material. May you have utmost confidence in God's promises and sufficiency to meet all your needs. May you be blessed with having many sincere loyal friends. May you be guided by the Holy Spirit in your daily life. May you be blessed with the joy of the Lord and have happiness in your soul. May the presence of the Lord be upon you as you pray. The greatest prayer is "Thy will be done." This statement is small in size but mighty in power. He is always there to bring you into His directed will.

Be marvelously blessed as He strengthens you to walk where He is guiding. He has given Himself to planning and studying what is best for you. Yield to Him and obey His Spirit. In Jesus Name.

ROOTED AND GROUNDED

Life is amazing when we look at it from God's standpoint. He has given 24 hours a day to serve Him in whatever way He leads you. His important requirement for happiness and peace is that you seek Him first every morning so He can direct your path for the day. And know that the Lord has set apart him that is godly for Himself. The Lord will hear when you call unto Him. May the Lord bless you more today than He did in the beginning.

"For thou, Lord, wilt bless the righteous; with favor wilt thou compass him as with a shield." Psalm 5:12

"Thou hast granted me life and favor, and thy visitation hath preserved my spirit." Job 10:12

May the Light of Christ shine upon your ways. May you dwell in safety and assurance in the Lord. May you be abundantly blessed and guided by the Holy Spirit. This in itself will promise to be a wonderful journey that will take you into many rich experiences if you will interpose Jesus in all that He leads you through. In Jesus Name.

TALK TO JESUS

Your simple life of devotion to God speaks louder than words, but moves heaven. Your relationship with the Lord is secured by His love. He has laid everything out in perfect order for you to walk every day with Him in simple faith. He directs you one step at a time. He holds out His hands to guide you through the maze of life and brings you through to live the ultimate life that He has chosen for you. In the Bible, David was a shepherd but God chose him to be king. Esther was an orphan, raised by her uncle, but God raised up this beautiful and devout girl, the choice of the king of Persia, to deliver her people from extinction. Your status in life does not matter to God. He looks at your heart.

Divine providence overrules all things and God's people are in His hands. God has chosen you for greatness to rule and reign with Jesus. Follow Him

"For ye see your calling, brethren, how that not many wise men after the flesh, not many mighty, not many noble are called: But God hath chosen the foolish things of the world to confound the wise; and God hath chosen the weak things of the world to confound the things which are mighty; And base things of the world, and things which are despised, hath God chosen, yea, and things which are not, to bring to nought things that are: That no flesh should glory in His presence." I Corinthians 1:26-29

You are wonderfully blessed and highly favored by the Lord. God is faithful, by whom you were called into the fellowship of Jesus. In Jesus Name.

TOUCH THE LORD

Early this morning, the Lord said, "When I look at them from heaven, I reach down and hold them in my arms. They are so precious to Me." And His love was like a light all around you.

"Thy mercy, O Lord, is in the heavens; and thy faithfulness reacheth unto the clouds.

Thy righteousness is like the great mountains; thy judgments are a great deep; O Lord, thou preservest man and beast. How excellent is thy loving-kindness, O God! Therefore the children of men put their trust under the shadow of thy wings. They shall be abundantly satisfied with the fatness of thy house; and thou shalt make them drink of the river of thy pleasures. For with thee is the fountain of life: in thy light shall we see light." Psalm 36:5-9

God is very merciful toward you and He is always faithful and always there for you. You can put your trust under the shadow of His wings and will be incredibly satisfied. Jesus said you will drink of the river of His pleasures. The fountain of life comes from the Lord. So be blessed with the deep and wonderful presence of Jesus. Purpose in your heart to get in touch with Jesus today. Prayer is insistence upon God's will being done. Press in and claim what is your special blessing today - that God's will is done. In Jesus Name.

RIGHTEOUSNESS BRINGS DELIVERANCE

May Jesus be the Lord of your life today. You are dead to sin but alive unto righteousness. May God give you a "winning" attitude. May He give you a glorious sense of confidence that you are an overcomer.

"For whatsoever is born of God overcometh the world: and this is the victory that overcometh the world, even our faith. Who is he that overcometh the world, but he that believeth that Jesus is the Son of God." I John 5:4-5

You are blessed of God to overcome all obstacles. He is your strength as you walk with the Lord in His gift of abundant life. God's word declares you are an overcomer. In Christ, you overcome the world, the flesh and the devil, by the blood of Jesus and the word of your testimony. God has given you abundant life and it flows to every organ of your body bringing healing and health. You have the mind of Christ for your thoughts today. He gives the ability to think clearly and make good judgments. Your mind is blessed with the spirit of wisdom, knowledge and understanding. All the "why this and why that" questions are gone under the blood of Jesus.

"I wisdom dwell with prudence, and find out knowledge of witty inventions." Proverbs 8:12

Blessings are upon your head. Godly blessings flow in your veins and you are revived in your spirit. In Jesus Name.

PASSIONATE PURSUIT OF GOD

May you walk with a passionate pursuit of God. He is the best thing that ever happened to you. When you welcome the Lord into all your circumstances, it is amazing how peaceful you are in your spirit. Strength from the Lord takes over and you no longer feel frazzled or anxious about things working out. Picture Jesus sitting beside you. Now lay all your problems one by one in the lap of Jesus and walk away. Release all your cares and anxieties. They are in the lap of Jesus and He will take care of your load and give you peace in your soul. He now will guide you in His wisdom. He will give you the mind of Christ and you will feel secure and safe because all your circumstances are in the hands of the Lord.

"Oh how great is thy goodness, which thou hast laid up for them that fear thee; which thou hast wrought for them that trust in thee before the sons of men; thou shalt hide them in the secret of thy presence from the pride of man: thou shalt keep them secretly in a pavilion from the strife of tongues. Blessed be the Lord: for He hath showed me His marvelous kindness in a strong city. O love the Lord, all ye His saints: for the Lord preserveth the faithful, and plentifully rewardeth the proud doer. Be of good courage, and He shall strengthen your heart, all ye that hope in the Lord." Psalm 31:19-21, 23-24

May the blessings of the Lord be poured out on your life and the grace, mercy, kindness and love of the Lord be upon you. In Jesus Name.

DESIRE WHAT GOD HAS

When your spirit is wounded, negative words that are spoken grab hold of that wounded area and pulls you into a place of self-protection and withdrawal from the Lord. But you are never too young or too old to be found. The Lord has provided a safe haven where He touches you and you are healed. Jesus is talking to God about you and unlimited love is surrounding you. They are looking at your heart and the sweet, perfect person they created you to be. There is a gentleness with the Lord. He is so kind. There is power in the way He kisses and hugs you without your awareness. May your attention be drawn to practicing gentleness, prayer and love.

"The Lord Jesus Christ be with thy spirit. Grace be with you. Amen."
II Timothy 4:22

May you be blessed with abounding blessings, having peace in your soul and joy in your heart. The Lord has touched you so may you make room for Him and look for Him with expectancy to come into your life in a new and wonderful way. In Jesus Name.

MOVING WITH THE LORD

Notice what you are reproducing in your life. If you say, "Watch me." What would they see? Would they see a beautiful pattern and example to follow? Would they understand that you have a true dedication to the Lord? God is releasing multiplication. Little will become much so you want to sow good deeds, with lots of love. To exhibit love, you must understand love. It is with love that evil is conquered. Love is life. Love is Christ.

"Watch ye, stand fast in the faith, quit you like men, be strong. Let all your things be done with charity." I Corinthians 16:13-14

May you enter into the season of increase. Barns are being built and filled for the future. Lift up your hearts to the Lord for Him to fill. Give Him your emptiness and watch the filling begin. There is no lack with God. Everything He has is yours. He has new levels of blessing for you. This is truth. Believe it. Let Him remove the old of the past. It no longer serves any purpose. It is hollow. Let Him go deep within you and pull out the old and replace it with the blessings He is holding out to you. This is a new day. There is healing in His wings.

"Because thou hast been my help, therefore in the shadow of thy wings will I rejoice. My soul followeth hard after thee: thy right hand upholdeth me." Psalm 63:7-8

All this is asked in the Name of Jesus.

LISTEN TO THE LORD

There is a group of people who walk with the presence of the Lord. The Lord speaks and they obey. They honor God with their lives. They are normal people who live in a normal world and do normal things, and they love the Lord. There is a peace about them that is quite impressive.

"My sheep hear my voice, and I know them, and they follow Me. And I give unto them eternal life; and they shall never perish, neither shall any man pluck them out of My hand. My Father, which gave them me, is greater than all; and no man is able to pluck them out of My Father's hand. I and My Father are one." John 10:27-30

Once the Lord saves your soul, you will forever be in the Lord's hand. So you live and move and have your being in God. He is always there. Let nothing rob you of the marvelous truth of His abiding presence.

May the Lord touch you today and make you whole. When He touches you, all that robs you of His very best will fall to the ground and you will walk away free of that coat of mail that has weighed you down. May the Lord speak from heaven to you and say, "Be free." His blessings are yours. His peace and provision are yours. The Lord's hand is on the doorknob that will open the door for you to walk into a whole new realm of wonderful living. In Jesus Name.

TRUST YOURSELF IN GOD'S HANDS

The Lord's hand is tenderly around you and holds you in the hollow of His hands. You are protected and loved by Him. He is your strength and your enabler. His ways are far above your ways and He desires to bring you into a whole new realm of holy living. He never desires for you to have second best because He paid the price for you to excel and succeed. He loves you enough to hold your hand as He guides you through the paths of life.

What do you ask of Him? Do you need guidance? He will guide you. Are you carrying a heavy load? His hands reach out to take it off you. Can you trust Him with all that concerns you? He is your greatest friend and no good thing will He withhold from you. He gives you riches and honor. His favor exceeds your highest expectation.

You are His responsibility to care for and bring you to an expected end. He will close the door to the whirlwind outside and will bring you into a closeness with Him where there is comfort and nurturing from His loving heart. He is healing your soul in ways you are not even aware of until one day you feel free and the air around you is fresh.

"Blessings are upon the head of the just. The blessing of the Lord, it maketh rich, and He addeth no sorrow with it." Proverbs 10:6, 22

"And ye shall know the truth, and the truth shall make you free.
"If the Son therefore shall make you free, ye shall be free indeed."
John 8:32, 36

The blessings of the Lord are real and active in your life. You are the called out ones and He will enable you to stand fast therefore in the liberty wherewith Christ has made you free. His high blessings are yours. Receive them by faith. In Jesus Name.

GOD DELIGHTS IN YOU

Jesus is the light of the world and the closer you live to Him the more your world is filled with light. Everything around you is covered with the light that comes from the presence of the Lord. Obedience to the Word of God always brings more light and more blessings. In all your ways acknowledge Him, and practice trusting and depending on Him. Know him intimately. Learn about who He really is.

The further you live from God who is light, the darker your world will be. Me, myself and I becomes the unholy trinity which is worshiped and put before the Lord. You become your own an idol which replaces the holy trinity being God, Jesus and the Holy Spirit.

The world was created for Jesus and all His creation. The bigger God is in your life the smaller your problems. Jesus covers them with His blood when you ask and trust Him. He saves you and cancels out your problems. He listens to every word you pray and answers with His divine intervention. He will hasten to help and will never fail you.

"Trust in the Lord with all thine heart; and lean not unto thine own understanding. In all thy ways acknowledge Him, and He shall direct thy paths. Be not wise in thine own eyes: fear the Lord, and depart from evil." Proverbs 3:5-7

May God's blessings be multiplied in your life and you are raised up into a new level of closeness with Him. In Jesus Name.

DELIVERANCE AND FREEDOM

There are some structures that must come down in your life for you to go where the Lord is taking you. Old mindsets, negative traditions that have passed down to you from your ancestors, old unbelief patterns, old hurts and wounds, old patterns of unforgiving, former lifestyles, all these are put under the blood of Jesus and you are no longer bothered or hindered from having God's best when these go. The Lord has promised that He will guard your life when He said, "I am with thee to deliver thee, saith the Lord."

Shackles that weigh you down are now put under the blood of Jesus and in their place is relief and clarity in your mind. Worry is replaced by trust and faith in the all-caring Christ who delivers you. Self-indulgence and bad habits can also rob you of God's best. Give it all to Jesus and He will free up your spirit. Put all that under the blood of Jesus that delivers you. Simply go steadily on with the Lord and He will cleanse you of the burdensome things that you have carried for many years. Let it all go. Release it all to the Lord. Allow Him to lift you up and out.

Life is not a treadmill that takes you aimlessly forward without any thought of direction. Step off the treadmill and walk purposely step by step where the Lord leads you. Let today be a new day of walking freely. Take a deep breath. Breathe in the breath of heaven that is clear and fresh and filled with new life. Trust the Lord every step of the way. You are a valuable treasure to Jesus and worthy of His loving care. He has time for you and will carry you through to freedom, happiness and fulfillment. This is sealed In Jesus Name.

"I can do all things through Christ which strengtheneth me.
But my God shall supply all your need according to His riches in glory by Christ Jesus." Philippians 4:13, 19

"Pray without ceasing." I Thessalonians 5:17

SEEK JESUS FIRST

"My kingdom is not of this world." John 18:36

There is a kingdom of God from which all your spiritual life will flow. And, there is a kingdom of this world from which the practical work flows. There is endless activity and attention given to the practical work. It seems to require it. But your reward in heaven is at risk when your time is consumed with the busy, hurry, "gotta do this" and "gotta do that" worldly kingdom stuff. It will take priority over your private time spent with the Lord.

Nothing truly satisfies your soul but Jesus. Once your spiritual foundation is laid on solid ground in the morning by prayer and Bible reading, you accomplish more things in a shorter time frame. Maintain the spiritual before the practical. Having a close relationship with Jesus is His greatest desire for you. Then you are settled in your spirit and satisfied in your heart. Getting rooted and grounded in God will keep you strong to stand tall. Always seek in prayer the kingdom of God first, and all these other things will be added to you.

"And, behold, I come quickly; and My reward is with Me, to give every man according as his work shall be." Revelation 22:12

The Lord bless you with a hunger and thirst for righteousness. May the Lord enable you to go all the way with Him. In Him is all fullness of joy and happiness. The Lord will heal and deliver you from anything that robs you of God's best. In Jesus Name.

GOD IS VERY REAL

"Mercy unto you, and peace, and love, be multiplied." Jude 2

May you be rich in faith and have no doubt. May your gaze be upward toward heaven where all grace abounds toward you, where life and wholeness in your spirit comes down from the Lord. He is Lord over all. Nothing can jostle you about or move against you to jar you. You are covered with the blood of Jesus and that is your protection. Pray and declare that Jesus is Lord over your life. You are hidden with Christ in God. Choose to live a holy and uncluttered life. Just praise the Lord. Thank Him that He is strong enough to keep you totally safe. The Lord will keep you in perfect peace when your mind thinks on Him. May He perfect everything that concerns you.

"Be ye therefore followers of God, as dear children; And walk in love, as Christ also hath loved us, and hath given Himself for us an offering and a sacrifice to God for a sweet-smelling savor." Ephesians 5:1-2

"Stand fast therefore in the liberty wherewith Christ hath made us free, and be not entangled again with the yoke of bondage." Galatians 5:1

Be wonderfully blessed and liberated to walk free in the Lord. In Jesus Name.

HOLD ONTO JESUS

We are living in such a fast-paced world today that very little time is left for you and Jesus to have time for fellowship. So take time and be watchful so that current distractions do not cause you to lose ground spiritually. You will have to take a stand and make an effort to maintain the ground you have gained. Keep your perspective and refuse to allow the enemy to get you off track. Preserving what you have is easier than regaining what you once obtained but lost.

"Now our Lord Jesus Christ Himself, and God, even our Father, which hath loved us, and hath given us everlasting consolation and good hope through grace, comfort your hearts, and establish you in every good word and work." II Thessalonians 2:16-17

"Cast not away therefore your confidence, which hath great recompense of reward." Hebrews 10:35

Be abundantly blessed with faith to believe God without doubting. May you be blessed with grace, mercy and peace from God your Father and Jesus Christ your Lord. In Jesus Name.

CLEANSED BY THE WORD

"Having therefore these promises dearly beloved, let us cleanse ourselves from all filthiness of the flesh and spirit, perfecting holiness in the fear of God." II Corinthians 7:1

We are to cleanse ourselves from all filthiness by refusing to walk in ungodliness. The flesh entails thinking good thoughts, refusing to think evil thoughts; speaking words that are acceptable before God; words that you could say to Jesus; living a clean life; yielding to the Lord in all things so that your spirit will be clean. If you have any doubt about doing something, do not do it, for whatsoever is not of faith is sin. Never allow yourself to be talked into making a choice. Always think clearly. Stand firm. Choose what God will bless. Never choose what pleases your flesh.

It is amazing how the look in your eyes and face will change when you cleanse yourself from all filthiness of the flesh and spirit. You will be more handsome, more beautiful. This is a proven fact. The meaning is to fulfill and accomplish completely a clean life. After Jesus cleanses us by His blood, we are to maintain a cleansed life that is pleasing to Him. You are cleansed by the washing of water by the Word.

"The Lord rewarded me according to my righteousness; according to the cleanness of my hands hath He recompensed me. For I have kept the ways of the Lord, and have not wickedly departed from my God. For all His judgments were before me: and as for His statutes, I did not depart from them. I was also upright before Him, and have kept myself from mine iniquity. Therefore the Lord hath recompensed me according to my righteousness; according to my cleanness in His eyesight." II Samuel 22:21-25

"Those that were clean escaped from them who live in error." II Peter 2:18

Be gloriously blessed and wonderfully encouraged in your God, for He loves you beyond limitations. In Jesus Name.

TAKE A STAND

The Lord gives a very direct word of how to receive His best:

"Be ye not unequally yoked together with unbelievers; for what fellowship hath righteousness with unrighteousness? and what communion hath light with darkness?

"And what concord hath Christ, with Belial? or what part hath he that believeth with an infidel?

And what agreement hath the temple of God with idols? for ye are the temple of the living God; as God hath said, I will dwell in them, and walk in them; and I will be their God, and they shall be my people." II Corinthians 6:14-16

May the impartation of strength from Jesus fill you with power in your inner man and His precious vibrant life live through you. Christ in you is your hope of glory. In Jesus Name.

ENCOURAGEMENT

"For I know the thoughts that I think toward you, saith the Lord, thoughts of peace, and not of evil, to give you an expected end. Then shall ye call upon Me, and ye shall go and pray unto Me, and I will hearken unto you. And ye shall seek Me, and find me, when ye shall search for Me with all your heart." Jeremiah 29:11-13

The windows of heaven are open to you to give you encouragement and peace. The Lord's desires for you are the best because He gives to you from His heart. His past time and entertainment is going about doing good. Everywhere He goes, goodness follows Him. He reaches out and touches you with His hand and healing follows. He speaks to you during the night season and you are pulled out of darkness into His glorious light. You pray and He answers. He establishes you with His presence.

Never loose faith in Jesus. He is there to bring you into an expected end filled with His marvelous light and blessings. You are blessed in the city, you are blessed in the field. Wherever you are and wherever you go you are blessed because you carry the anointed One, Jesus the Christ, in your heart.

"And out of them shall proceed thanksgiving and the voice of them that make merry: and I will multiply them, and they shall not be few: I will also glorify them, and they shall not be small." Jeremiah 30:19

Pray this scripture over yourself every day for thirty days and see the good changes that will come about in your life. Be abundantly blessed. In Jesus Name.

PROMOTION

You were made for success. Think deeply about this. Encourage yourself in the Lord and believe His Word about you. David was a shepherd watching over his flock of sheep in a field. Samuel came to his father and said, "God showed me that one of your sons will be Israel's next king." Six of his sons were brought before Samuel and he said, "Do you have another son?" And when David was brought out of the field, Samuel said, "He is the one."

In an instant, David went from being a shepherd to being Israel's king. He will do the same for you. Promotion comes from the Lord. You have God's approval when You are submissive to God first. May favor from God and man surround you like a shield.

"Thou wilt keep him in perfect peace whose mind is stayed on thee; because he trusteth in thee.

Trust ye in the Lord forever; for in the Lord JEHOVAH is everlasting strength." Isaiah 26:3-4

May the Lord bless you with His perfect will and open many doors of opportunity for you to prosper. When you are called of God, every force at His disposal will work for you. In Jesus Name.

MARVELOUS CREATION

May the Lord reveal to you who you really are. He wants you to know who He made you to be. He looked at your life from beginning to end, and He made you perfect. He wants you to be you. Sometimes you have to get alone and meditate on this - maybe more than once. You are not complicated. He thought of this beautiful, wonderful person and He created you. He did not make you to live a life of confusion, or a life of insecurity, or striving to be someone other than who He made you to be. He made you rock-solid, because you were made in the image of God.

You need never compare yourself with another person. Compare yourself to Jesus only. God never compared you to anyone. He only makes originals. No one in the world is like you. He made you a fresh, new, exciting, simply perfect creation formed by His own hands. He gave you two beautiful eyes so you could see all the beauty of the earth He created you to live in. The earth is the Lord's and the fullness thereof. He created the lilies of the field who toil not, neither do they struggle. Are you not much better than they?

"And yet I say unto you, that even Solomon in all his glory was not arrayed like one of these lilies." Matthew 6:29

May you be tremendously blessed by understanding who you really are. When you do, new strength of awareness will sweep into your soul and you will be transformed overnight. Your eyes will suddenly see what God has wanted to show you all along. You will be so confident in God that no evil words or accusations will have any effect on you, not ever. You are founded upon the rock Christ Jesus who forever sustains you. In Jesus Name.

GOOD CONSCIENCE

After attending my son, Phillip's, graduation ceremony where he received a degree for his accomplishments in college, the thought came that "this is how it will be in heaven when we stand before the Lord and give an account of ourselves to God."

Most importantly, what did we do with Jesus? How much of our life did we give to Him? How obedient were we to His Word? Did we give Him honor and respect to yield to Him? His hand was always extended to us with many blessings. He always wants the best for us. Did we yield to His righteousness?

"Be not deceived; God is not mocked: for whatsoever a man soweth, that shall he also reap. For he that soweth to his flesh shall of the flesh reap corruption; but he that soweth to the Spirit shall of the Spirit reap life everlasting." Galatians 6:7-8

"But we are bound to give thanks always to God for you, brethren beloved of the Lord, because God hath from the beginning chosen you to salvation through sanctification of the Spirit, and belief of the truth: Whereunto He called you by our gospel, to the obtaining of the glory of our Lord Jesus Christ." II Thessalonians 2:13-14

The Lord wants to bless you abundantly so that you will have the glory of Jesus on your life. You receive blessing when you stand fast in what you have been taught, by the Word of God. The Lord, Himself, has loved you, and given you everlasting consolation and good hope through grace, comforting your heart, and establishing and strengthening you in every good word and work. This is the blessing passed down to you. In Jesus Name.

JESUS SEES YOU

In a documentary mini series called "Against All Odds" a remarkable story is told about an Israeli platoon who found themselves in the midst of a minefield along the Syrian border during the Yom Kippur War. When the platoon realized they were in a minefield they pulled out their bayonets and started to dig out mines and disarm them. Suddenly, a fierce wind began to blow, removing the sand from the minefield. Each and every mine was exposed and the soldiers ventured through the minefield unscathed.

"Be merciful unto me, O God, be merciful unto me: for my soul trusteth in thee: yea, in the shadow of thy wings will I make my refuge, until these calamities be overpast." Psalm 57:1

God's word, which is your daily spiritual bread of life, and His Spirit equips you thoroughly for life and godliness. Being obedient to His word and abiding in His Spirit you can avoid every deadly trap of the enemy. God blows upon your path with a fierce wind. He will quicken a scripture to your heart that will be like a voice from heaven guiding you along the path to safety. It is the voice of the Lord that speaks quietly and deeply into your spirit. Sometimes it may seem like "just a thought," when it is actually the Lord quietly talking to you.

When Terry Lee, my nephew, was a small boy playing in the back yard, Bon, his mother, saw a guide wire from a telephone pole break and it would have fallen on Terry Lee, when Bon yelled, "Run, Terry Lee, run." He instantly obeyed his mother and ran to safety. The Lord saved his life. So it is that God who sits on a throne in heaven, sees all around you, and when you are about to walk into danger, He yells into your spirit, "Run, run to safety." Obedience to His voice will save you from a lot of misery. He calls you into His realm of safety, where no harm can touch you.

May His many powerful blessings come into your life and you feel safe and secure in Jesus' loving arms. In Jesus Name.

JESUS THE HEALER

The windows of heaven are open over you, and the blessings are being poured out. Concentrate on Jesus for it is through Him that all blessings flow. We make declaration that everything in you is blessed. God's healing power is working in your life and every part of your body, mind, soul, spirit and heart is made whole for "By the stripes of Jesus, you are healed."

"Looking unto Jesus, the Author and Finisher of our faith." Hebrews 12:2

The Lord wants His people well. He wants you blessed with a joyful and happy attitude. May His resurrection life raise you up to live victoriously over all the cares of life. God has shielded you with His grace. May you believe His precious promises by faith and enter into a whole new realm of standing-on-the-Word-of-God faith. Through Christ, you are exalted above all these cares. You are established by faith that God is presently working for you. Why? Because He loves you with an unconditional love that follows you wherever you may go. He never leaves you. He never forsakes you. At the end of every day, you will realize that the Lord was with you every step of the way. There is a mighty God guiding you. You will never lose your way. He has been there all the time

"Let them shout for joy, and be glad, that favor My righteous cause: yea, let them say continually, Let the Lord be magnified, which hath pleasure in the prosperity of His servant. And my tongue shall speak of thy righteousness and of thy praise all the day long." Psalm 35:27-28

May you receive this blessing from the Lord. In Jesus Name.

TRUST JESUS

When you draw near to God, you cease asking for things. He already knows what you need before you ask. You draw near to God so that you may get to know Him. He is your pattern to live in excellence. God's excellence of living is above the world's standards. Living in close relationship with the Lord will give you everything you need. He fills the void places. He drives out all darkness and gives you light. His Spirit loosens you from the beggarly elements of the world and you see with new vision, you live with new hope, you excel to greater heights. Seek Him. Seek His will for your life. His desires for you will always bring you higher and bring you closer to the radiant light of Christ that fills you to overflow with the best. When this happens, your wants and self-desires are as nothing compared to what He has for you.

"This then is the message which we have heard of him, and declare unto you, that God is light, and in Him is no darkness at all. If we say that we have fellowship with Him, and walk in darkness, we lie, and do not the truth. But if we walk in the light, as He is in the light, we have fellowship one with another, and the blood of Jesus Christ His Son cleanses us from all sin." I John 1:5-7

May the hand of the Lord be upon you and bless you in wonderful ways. When you are in touch with God, you are the door through which He can reach your entire household. Just as the Dad is responsible to God for the care of his family, so is the believer responsible for his relatives to find Christ as Savior. Stay before the Lord in prayer and you will see everyone of your loved ones saved. In Jesus Name.

HOLY SPIRIT'S WORK

"Likewise the Spirit also helpeth our infirmities; for we know not what we should pray for as we ought; but the Spirit itself maketh intercession for us with groanings which cannot be uttered. And He that searcheth the hearts knoweth what is the mind of the Spirit, because He maketh intercession for the saints according to the will of God." Romans 8:26

Jesus, the great Intercessor, sits at the right hand of God making intercession for you 24-hours a day, and if God be for you, who can be against you. God gave His Son to die on a cross for you so how shall He not freely give you all things. The blessings of God are upon you. He loves you.

"Who is he that condemneth. It is Christ that died, yea rather, that is risen again, who is even at the right hand of God, who also maketh intercession for us. Who shall separate us from the love of Christ? shall tribulation, or distress, or persecution, or famine, or nakedness, or peril, or sword? Nay, in all these things we are more than conquerors through Him that loved us." Romans 8:34-35, 37

Nothing shall be able to separate you from the love of God, which is in Christ Jesus your Lord. You are blessed forever.

You belong to Him. You are His children who are blessed with all the blessings that are in Jesus. He wants to bless you with all things. He chose you before the foundation of the world. He saw your life from beginning to end, and He chose you. He trusts you. There was no condition that you should have any natural ability. It is Christ Himself that He puts into your heart that matters. You are saved by the blood of Jesus and eternally His. Reach up and touch Him. In Jesus Name.

REVIVE THE INSPIRATION

"Thou hast granted me life and favor; and thy visitation has pre-served my spirit." Job 10:12

May the Lord revive the inspiration that came into your spirit when He first touched you when you were younger. Once He touches you, He never lifts His hand from your life. In the passing of time, that experience of divine inspiration may have become buried some-where in your spirit. Yet He has never left you. His presence on you today is as miraculous as it was the day He saved your soul and brought you out of sin into abundant life as a son/daughter of God. May the Lord bring a renewed flourishing of the glorious inspiration of God that will fill your heart to overflow with new life and new vision that brings you into His ultimate divine destiny.

"Stand fast, therefore, in the liberty wherewith Christ hath made us free, and be not entangled again with the yoke of bondage." Galatians 5:1

The word "entangled" denotes that somewhere along the line, you have "held in" a grudge against someone because of a quarrel. Release that feeling to the Lord and be free. Return to the liberty wherewith Christ will make you free again. There is freedom through Christ's death on the cross and His resurrection to walk in newness of life. Never be a slave to sin again.

May the Lord's ultimate blessings be upon you for you are truly the chosen ones whom the Lord has blessed. In Jesus Name.

TURN TO THE LORD

"Therefore say thou unto them, Thus saith the Lord of hosts, Turn ye unto me, saith the Lord of hosts, and I will turn unto you, saith the Lord of hosts." Zechariah 1:3

Turning to the Lord in good times and not so good times means He is always there for you. The picture is that He is sitting waiting for as many as will to turn to Him. When you do, you will find that He is the all-sufficient One who meets you where you are and will talk to you about whatever is on your mind. He will sit and listen without interruption and He not only hears your words but He sees your heart and understands how deep your feelings go with every word you speak. And then He answers. He will talk to you from the standpoint of having full understanding of the importance of your words but also the hidden need. Just take time to listen. You will no doubt hear words from Him that touches your soul.

In the Hebrew language, every letter has seven meanings and every word has 70 meanings. So that means every three letter word has 91 meanings.

In your cry for help, God hears the word "help," sees the depth of the help you need, understands what has happened that caused you to cry out to Him, has knowledge of what affected you to cry out for help and in answering your prayer, meets all your needs. So the Lord says, "Turn ye unto Me." Simple words but powerful meaning.

"For the Word of God is quick, and powerful, and sharper than any two-edged sword, piercing even to the dividing asunder of soul and spirit, and of the joints and marrow, and is a discerner of the thoughts and intents of the heart." Hebrews 4:12

May blessings from heaven flow into the very depths of your soul with healing and resurrection life. In Jesus Name.

GOOD NAME

May you obtain a good report from everyone. May your name be honored by those who hear about you. May only goodness follow your name and reputation wherever you are mentioned. May your eyes be fixed on Jesus who strengthens you to make good choices that your name be not shamed.

Love is your greatest ally. When you act in love from your heart, it will affect your whole life and you will be remembered by your love. Protecting your good name is to get rightly related to the Lord and then to your fellow men.

"If it be possible, as much as lieth in you, live peaceably with all men." Romans 12:18

"By this I know that thou favorest me, because mine enemy doth not triumph over me." Psalm 41:11

"And the whole multitude sought to touch Him: for there went virtue out of Him, and healed them all." Luke 6:19

Look at the significance of the Name of Jesus:

"And whatsoever ye do in word or deed, do all in the name of the Lord Jesus, giving thanks to God and the Father by Him." Colossians 3:17

May multiplied blessings be on your life every day. Always keep your eyes on Jesus. In Jesus Name.

FAITH IS BELIEVING GOD

"Faith cometh by hearing and hearing by the Word of God." Romans 10:17

"Without faith it is impossible to please Him." Hebrews 11:6

So you receive long-living faith by hearing and reading the Word of God. As you soak in God's Word, the blessings come as the righteousness of God is revealed to you. Doubt will lift off you as your faith in the righteous God increases. Then you will enter into liberty and freedom where the Spirit of the Lord is.

The Spirit gives life, even abundant life, transforming life, radiant life, overcoming life. Your appearance changes. The grief, the turmoil, the look of anxiety leaves your face and you have a brand new look. Christ is becoming more real and He is filling up all the hollow places inside you with His glorious presence. And you are changed into the same image of Christ from glory to glory. May you be blessed with a new-found, new-created confidence and assurance and self-awareness that will give you more happiness than you can imagine. You are truly the blessed of the Lord. In Jesus Name.

YOU ARE JESUS' INHERITANCE

May the sweet presence of Jesus move upon your heart, mind, soul, spirit and body and give you heavenly peace. All the bustle of life, the clamor for your time, the hurrying here and there, settles down when you reach up and take hold of the hands of Jesus. He will carry you through. He will lift you up. He will bless you because He is personally watching over your life. He protects and loves you.

It is Jesus who is the same yesterday, today, and forever. He holds you in the hollow of His hand. You are precious to Him. You have great value. He died for you to live an overcoming life. He made a world and put you in it and trusts you to take care of His business. He trusts you to make a better world by letting your light shine for Him. You are glorious to Him. You were created by the hands of Jesus, and you are beautiful in His sight.

"Therefore, my beloved brethren, be ye steadfast, unmovable, always abounding in the work of the Lord, forasmuch as ye know that your labor is not in vain in the Lord." I Corinthians 15:58

God is desiring to use you mightily in His service. There is a new dawn awakening where old things are passed away and behold all things are become new. Reach up and touch the Lord. He is waiting for you. In Jesus Name.

KNOW JESUS AND BELIEVE

"For Ye were sometimes darkness, but now are ye light in the Lord: walk as children of light: For the fruit of the Spirit is in all goodness and righteousness and truth; Proving what is acceptable unto the Lord. And have no fellowship with the unfruitful works of darkness, but rather reprove them." Ephesians 5:8-11

The blessing of the Lord falls upon those who walk in the light of Christ; goodness, righteousness and truth. The abundant life is a Spirit-filled life. Under God's control, you are strengthened by His love for you. If you really listen to Him and accept instruction about Him, then you learn that Jesus instills truth in you. Then so far as your former way of life is concerned, you must strip off your old nature, because your old nature is thoroughly rotted by its deceptive desires, and you must let your spirits and minds keep being renewed, and clothe yourselves with the new nature created to be godly, which expresses itself in the righteousness and holiness that flow from the truth. So imitate God, as His dear children, and live a life of love.

Lord, may all these precious ones yield themselves to Your goodness and righteousness and truth. May they continually be blessed and strengthened with all the power of Christ that comes from Your glorious might. In Jesus Name.

CROWNED WITH GLORY

"There is none holy as the Lord: for there is none besides thee: neither is there any rock like our God." I Samuel 2:2

May you go to God about everything by seeking and asking in prayer. Trust Him. Draw spiritual life from Him. Put everything in the lap of the Lord. He loves you so much. May you have the mind of Christ. Bringing the Lord into your everyday life is so natural when you belong to Him. May you seek the Lord's will and become more involved with Him. Listen to the voice of the Savior, the still quiet voice. In the Bible, Samuel heard God's voice when he was just a small boy before his ears had been dulled by earth's sounds. A child's heart and ears naturally hear the Lord. May the Lord speak to your inner heart and ear.

"Thou hast loved righteousness and hated iniquity; therefore God, even thy God, hath anointed thee with the oil of gladness above thy fellows." Hebrews 1:9

Trusting that the wonderful blessings of His presence rest upon you. May the power and anointing of the Holy Spirit lead you into the total fullness of Christ. Fullness means: covered over with Christ, completely assured by Christ, cram full and level up the hollow places with Christ, satisfied by Christ, finish, entirely accomplish, to carry out fully, most surely believe, and fully know Jesus. You are completely blessed when you are filled with all the fullness of God. In Jesus Name.

GOD IS USING YOU

"Be perfect, be of good comfort, be of one mind, live in peace; and the God of love and peace shall be with you. The grace of the Lord Jesus Christ, and the love of God, and the communion of the Holy Spirit, be with you all. Amen." II Corinthians 13:11, 14

May you be blessed by keeping your eyes on Jesus who is your rock and shield and comforter. Seek the Lord with love in your heart. Lay all self-sufficiency at the cross and lean on the wisdom and discernment of the Holy Spirit. May you abound in every good work. The Lord is reaching out to draw you higher so you can know Him better and walk worthy of God, who has called you into His kingdom and glory.

Read the Word and let it bless and strengthen you in your inner man. May you seek to please the Lord so you can be an example of the believers, in word, in conversation, in your manner of life, in love, in spirit, in faith, and in purity.

May you seriously pursue Jesus - not seeking great things for yourself - but losing forever putting yourself before Him. That means, dying to self and all selfish desires that would take you away from the destiny of God. Let Him take you into His purpose. You were created for a divine purpose, singled out by God, and no one else can fill that place. Tremendous blessings are there for you every day. Ask and you shall receive. In Jesus Name.

KNOW JESUS

The Lord's hand of mercy and blessing is reaching out to you. He is God over all and His strength is there for you. His strength becomes your strength. His joy and peace becomes yours to have every day. The Lord is longing for you to call out to Him for everything you need. He is there to answer your prayer. Serve Him with a perfect heart and with a willing mind: for the Lord searches all hearts, and understands all the imaginations of your thoughts. If you seek Him, He will be found of you. May His love overflow your life. He is full of compassion and grace. May you tap into His abundance that is waiting for you.

"Salvation belongeth to the Lord: thy blessing is upon thy people." Psalm 3:8

"But know that the Lord hath set apart him that is godly for Himself: the Lord will hear when I call unto Him." Psalm 4:3

Seek Jesus. Get to know Him. Spend time with Him. Always pray and do not grow weary. The Holy Spirit will guide you into precious communion with Him and the more you know Jesus, the stronger you will be in every area of your life. You are to be transformed daily into the likeness of Him.

Be abundantly blessed by always walking worthy of God. In Jesus Name.

RECEIVE MORE

May the Lord begin working marvelous signs and wonders among each of you and manifest His mighty power that none can doubt it was truly the hand of God. There is no limitation with Him, and it is His will to begin doing powerful things that will truly draw your eyes toward Him, in whom are hid all the treasures of wisdom and knowledge.

"If ye then be risen with Christ, seek those things which are above, where Christ sitteth on the right hand of God.

"Set your affection on things above, not on things on the earth.

"And above all these things put on charity, which is the bond of perfectness.
And let the peace of God rule in your hearts, to the which also ye are called in one body; and be ye thankful. Let the Word of Christ dwell in you richly in all wisdom; teaching and admonishing one another in psalms and hymns and spiritual songs, singing with grace in your hearts to the Lord." Colossians 3:1-2, 14-16

May you be gloriously blessed with an understanding of the love of Jesus. May your eyes be open to the significance of the risen Christ and you receive into your spirit the understanding of how to effectively walk in wisdom before God. In Jesus Name.

SURROUNDED BY JESUS

May the powerful Words of Jesus surround your lives, homes, jobs, schools, cars, and all your possessions. May the blood of Jesus protect you from all harm in body, mind, soul, spirit, heart and emotions, thoughts, intelligence, creative abilities, your eyes to see with your spirit, your ears to hear what the Holy Spirit is saying, your mouth to speak words of wisdom, and have the mind of Christ. There is no power in hell that can touch you for you are the children of the most high God and it is in Him that you are hidden. We declare peace be all around you and you be blessed with the light of Jesus that will manifest, and you will see it in the time of need. May you be enveloped with the love of Jesus.

"He that dwells in the secret place of the Most High shall abide under the shadow of the Almighty." Psalm 91:1

May you be gloriously blessed by a touch of the Lord's hand. May you be filled with holy love that loves everyone, the good and the bad. May you be clothed with His glory and whatever you do in word or deed, do all in the name of the Lord Jesus with a thankful heart. In Jesus Name.

PRAYER IN THE THICKET

"Trust in Him at all times; ye people, pour out your heart before him: God is a refuge for us." Psalm 62:8

Early African believers were earnest and regular in private devotions. Each one reportedly had a separate spot in the thicket where he would pour out his heart to God. Over time, the paths to these places became well worn. As a result, if one of these believers began to neglect prayer, it was soon apparent to the others. They would kindly remind the negligent one, "Brother, the grass grows on your path."

Prayer is a time when we can be completely intimate with the Lord. We can share all our burdens, heartaches, situations and life struggles, but sometimes we need to get away into the thicket, alone, and gaze intently at the things unseen where the secrets of God are made known. The Lord loves to be intimate with us. He does not want a superficial relationship of recited prayers, but a deep relationship with Him - the One who loves us with a love that is everlasting.

Prayer is the first thing to be pushed aside and we do not have time for. But God says, "Pray without ceasing." I Thessalonians 5:17

You will have to set the seemingly "important" things aside and take time to pray. The Spirit within you will pray through you and things will start to happen that will fulfill God's purposes. Always pray in Jesus Name. Simply obey and pray.

May you be abundantly blessed as you give yourself to prayer. In Jesus Name.

BREAKTHROUGHS

You are blessed with incredible breakthroughs. The Lord is going before you and pulling down the powers that have prevented you from having God's best. He wants you to excel spiritually so that you will have a greater span of blessing in what He has called you to do. There is so much more. As you press in to hear the heart of God, He is going to show you magnificent ways of breaking free of the old and walking with the new blessings He has for you. May you yield yourselves to His ways and no longer yield to worldly desires.

"I delight to do thy will, O my God." Psalm 40:8

"Blessed are the meek: for they shall inherit the earth.

"Blessed are they which do hunger and thirst after righteousness: for they shall be filled.

"Blessed are the merciful: for they shall obtain mercy.

"Blessed are the pure in heart: for they shall see God.

"Blessed are the peacemakers: for they shall be called the children of God." Matthew 5:5-9

The greatest things and those which bring the most glory to God are yet to be revealed and yet to be done. May you be blessed to hear the quiet voice of the Holy Spirit that will always lead you into peace and quietness of heart.

In Jesus Name.

GOD'S LABORERS

"This is a faithful saying, and these things I will that thou affirm constantly, that they which have believed in God might be careful to maintain good works. These things are good and profitable unto men." Titus 3:8

There is a blessing upon the obedient ones who maintain good works. Rarely are good works forgotten by those you are kind to. There was a man who always smiled. Even his eyes smiled. He was remembered for this quality. Just the act of being pleasant is a good work. My best friend passed away today, and one of the things she is remembered by is that she was so kind and loving to my Mother. Let us consider one another to provoke unto love and to good works. God is raising you up to be a powerful blessing to others as you let the love of Jesus shine through your works. People need love. They need your thoughtfulness and kindness.

"If ye fulfill the royal law according to the scripture, Thou shalt love thy neighbor as thyself, ye do well." James 2:8

Royal means regal, sovereign, preeminent law.

"Follow peace with all men, and holiness, without which no man shall see the Lord." Hebrews 12:14

"Now the God of peace, that brought again from the dead our Lord Jesus, that great shepherd of the sheep, through the blood of the everlasting covenant,

"Make you perfect in every good work to do His will, working in you that which is well-pleasing in His sight, through Jesus Christ; to whom be glory forever and ever." Hebrews 13:20-21

Be marvelously blessed with the Lord's sweet presence and precious favor on your life. In Jesus Name.

CLOSE TO JESUS

Blessings, blessings, blessings be upon you. The hand of the Lord is upon all them for good that seek Him. He has extended mercy and grace to you and you shall be strengthened as the hand of the Lord your God is upon you. He is continually doing a work in you to conform you into the image of Jesus. As you consecrate your all to Him, He will use you to be a bright light in a world of darkness. You shine like stars in the hand of the Lord.

"Let no corrupt communication proceed out of your mouth, but that which is good to the use of edifying, that it may minister grace unto the hearers.
And grieve not the Holy Spirit of God, whereby you are sealed unto the day of redemption. Let all bitterness, and wrath, and anger, and clamor, and evil speaking, be put away from you, with all malice. And be ye kind one to another, tenderhearted, forgiving one another, even as God for Christ's sake hath forgiven you." Ephesians 4:29-32

"Be ye therefore followers of God, as dear children; And walk in love, as Christ also hath loved us." Ephesians 5:1-2

May the love of the Lord well up in your soul and flood your life with peace and joy. May the thoughts in your mind and the words that you speak be pleasing to the Lord. In Jesus Name.

GOD ENABLES

May the Lord give you knowledge and skill in all learning with • wisdom. May the Lord lift your hearts to know God's ways and follow Him. May you purpose in your heart that you would not defile yourself with the ways of the world, but wholly lean on the righteousness of the Lord to carry you through.

"Thou art my portion, O Lord: I have said that I would keep thy words. I entreated thy favor with my whole heart: be merciful unto me according to thy word. I thought on my ways, and turned my feet unto thy testimonies." Psalm 119:57-59

"How sweet are thy words unto my taste! yea, sweeter than honey to my mouth. Through thy precepts I get understanding: therefore I hate every false way." Psalm 103-104

You are blessed of the Lord and highly favored. No good thing will He withhold from those who walk uprightly with Him. The joy of the Lord is your strength, and happy is that people, whose God is the Lord. The Lord takes pleasure in His people, and He will beautify the meek with salvation. Let the high praises of God be in your mouth. He makes peace in your borders and fills you with the finest of His blessings.

May the Lord take you in His arms and show you how abundantly blessed you are. You are greatly loved and His favor is upon you. In Jesus Name.

SOAR LIKE AN EAGLE

"For who is God, save the Lord? And who is a rock, save our God? God is my strength and power; and He maketh my way perfect. He maketh my feet like hinds' feet; and setteth me upon my high places. He teacheth my hands to war; so that a bow of steel is broken by mine arms. Thou hast also given me the shield of thy salvation; and thy gentleness hath made me great. Thou hast enlarged my steps under me; so that my feet did not slip. He is the tower of salvation for his king: and showeth mercy to His anointed, unto David, and to his seed forevermore." II Samuel 22:32-37, 51

The security you have in the Lord is so sure and so powerfully protective. The Lord stands behind His Word and performs all the promises that you claim as being yours. You can ask for the light of Christ to come into your life and He answers by driving out all darkness. You ask for health, and His reply is, "I am the God who heals you."

May Jesus who died for you give you resurrection life and restore all your desire to stretch toward your destiny. May He restore all your hidden talents, give you faith to reach out and take hold of the hem of His garment and be instantly healed from any and all limitations. You are wonderfully blessed with awesome credentials. You have been blessed with gifts and talents that have never been tapped into. May visions and the Lord's miraculous works begin to be manifested in your life. Believe God for the anointing to fulfill all your dreams. In Jesus precious Name.

DAWNING OF A NEW DAY

There is a new day dawning. In the world, wickedness is abounding more and more until Jesus returns. But for those who have been saved and belong to Jesus, the future is becoming brighter and brighter. As you draw close to the Lord, you are going to see more of heaven's plan and purpose than ever before. Jesus is going to become more real to you. He is a real, living person who sits beside God in heaven and is the epitome of power and love and tenderness which is in His heart toward you.

He is strengthening you to come closer to Him so He can wash away all that clutters your mind and life. The freedom that He gives is yours. He will direct you to follow Him as you walk less encumbered with unnecessary burdens. He is watching over you and desires that Christ be formed in you every day.

"For ye are all the children of God by faith in Christ Jesus." Galatians 3:26

"My little children, of whom I travail in birth again until Christ be formed in you." Galatians 4:19

May you follow that which is good by abstaining from all appearance of evil.

May God do a mighty work in you and give you peace. May your whole spirit and soul and body be kept blameless until the coming of our Lord Jesus Christ. He is faithful that called you, who also will accomplish His will in your life. May your heart be stirred to read the Word, pray, obey, and yield completely to the Lord. In Jesus Name.

POWER OF SALVATION

Once you accept Jesus Christ as your personal Savior, you are transformed from a sinner to a child of God. You no longer run with the crowd and live in sin and worldliness. Christ put His Spirit in you and Christ is now the love of your life, your King of Kings and Lord of Lords. You belong to Jesus and you now are to give yourself to prayer, reading your Bible to gain knowledge and wisdom, so that you will understand what godliness is all about.

You are a new creature in Christ. From now on, you will be able to call upon Him in prayer about everything you need. His promises in the Bible are yours to claim and believe. You have changed. Christ is in you and is your hope of glory. You have exchanged the garments of the world and you now are clothed with heavenly garments. There are so many experiences that you will have and they all will work for your good so that you will become more and more like Jesus.

"Wherefore seeing we also are compassed about with so great a cloud of witnesses, let us lay aside every weight, and the sin which doth so easily beset us, and let us run with patience the race that is set before us,

"Looking unto Jesus the author and finisher of our faith; who for the joy that was set before him endured the cross, despising the shame, and is set down at the right hand of the throne of God." Hebrews 12:1-2

May the strength of Jesus fill your body to stand tall in God. May you hold to the course of holiness and righteousness, and willingly yield and obey the Word of God so that you will be the bright light among the darkness of this world. Always maintain a spirit of humility that comes when you serve Jesus with your whole heart and not serve yourself. In Jesus Name.

RUGGED CROSS

All the wonderful benefits that we have as believers came at an enormous cost to God. He gave His only Son to be crucified on a rugged cross and put all the wicked sins of the world from Adam to the sins of the last person to be born, upon Jesus who became sin for us, though He was spotless, never committed any sin, and was totally holy. Our sins are forgiven only by the sacrificial death of Jesus and by His blood that came from His hands and feet and side when they nailed Him to His cross. Forgiveness of sin did not come easy. God could not forgive sin because He is a holy God who cannot look upon sin. It took Jesus on the cross to give us forgiveness, salvation, healing, deliverance and the hope of being in heaven with Him throughout eternity.

By Jesus dying on the cross, satan was totally defeated, stripped of all power he once had and is destined to a lake of fire world without end. When God raised Jesus from the dead, He rose in total triumphant victory over death, hell and the grave. The only way sin and satan exists today is by deception and lies. He is the father of lies. But he is totally defeated by Jesus.

"Submit yourselves therefore to God. Resist the devil, and he will flee from you.

"Draw nigh to God, and He will draw nigh to you. Cleanse your hands, ye sinners, and purify your hearts, ye double-minded.

"Be afflicted, and mourn, and weep: let your laughter be turned to mourning, and your joy to heaviness.

"Humble yourselves in the sight of the Lord, and He shall lift you up." James 4:7-10

"Come now, and let us reason together, saith the Lord; though your sins be as scarlet, they shall be as white as snow; though they be red like crimson, they shall be as wool." Isaiah 1:18

May you receive His miraculous blessing of repentance and forgiveness, thanking God for His incredible gift of living your life apart from the evil works of the world. You will live in the world, but are not to partake of the evil that is in the world. In Jesus Name.

ONE HOUR

One hour alone with the Lord in prayer will change your life. There is something about spending time in the presence of God that transcends all else. It is there that you can pour out all that is in your heart and He hears every word, every emotion behind your words, feels all your hurt, all your joy, all your exhaustion, all your confusion. You take each need and put it in the lap of the Lord. He sits there holding everything you have prayed and at your last "Amen," you walk away light and airy with a bounce in your step and Jesus stands up holding every word you have said, smiles, and walks away with it. That is what one hour alone with Him will do for you.

Then to read even one chapter in your Bible feeds your soul and gives you inner strength for the day.

"And when they looked, they saw that the stone was rolled away: for it was very great." Mark 16:4

The stone of your heavy burdens is rolled away when you pray.

"And the glory which thou gavest Me I have given them; that they may be one, even as we are one." John 17:22

May the Lord bless you with His life-changing touch and lift you higher and higher in Him In Jesus Name.

JESUS IS COMING BACK

My apartment faces the east and when I awoke this morning looking into the eastern sky saying good morning to the Lord, the thought came to me, "One day we will see Jesus standing in the sky with His hands outstretched drawing all of us up to Him." What a glorious day that will be to see Jesus face to face.

"For the Lord Himself shall descend from heaven with a shout, with the voice of the archangel, and with the trump of God: and the dead in Christ shall rise first: Then we which are alive and remain shall be caught up together with them in the clouds, to meet the Lord in the air: and so shall we ever be with the Lord. Wherefore comfort one another with these words." I Thessalonians 4:16, 17

So let our attention be drawn upward, putting on Christ every day, yielding to the Holy Spirit, doing good works, forsaking the sin of this world, abstaining from all appearance of evil. Get ready to meet the Lord in the air.

"And the very God of peace sanctify you wholly; and I pray God your whole spirit and soul and body be preserved blameless unto the coming of our Lord Jesus Christ. Faithful is He that calleth you, who also will do it." I Thessalonians 5:23-24

Father, hold these precious ones close to your heart. Radiate Your love into their spirits. Comfort them. Encourage them. Give them newness of life. Renew a right spirit in them. Soften their hearts one toward another. Bless them with your holy blessings. In Jesus Name.

FOLLOW ME

"Follow Me," Jesus said.

This is the way He called His twelve disciples to follow Him. He simply passed by the person, said "Follow Me," and they followed. Jesus did not plead, He did not ask the second time, He did not wait to see what their response would be, He simply said, "Follow Me." And their response was immediate. They laid down what they were doing and followed Jesus.

"And as He passed by, He saw Levi the son of Alphaeu sitting at the receipt of custom, and said unto him, Follow Me. And he arose and followed Him." Mark 2:14

May the Lord speak to your heart to follow Him and you instantly obey. He has so many marvelous things He wants you to do for Him. Stand for the Lord where you are and then branch out to walk where Jesus leads you. May the anointing of the Holy Spirit be upon your life and you become a powerful and obedient servant of the Lord. May blessings unlimited be upon you.

In Jesus Name.

DEDICATED LIFE

"And the Lord make you to increase and abound in love one toward another, and toward all men, even as we do toward you: To the end He may stablish your hearts unblamable in holiness before God, even our Father, at the coming of our Lord Jesus Christ with all His saints." I Thessalonians 3:12

As you are guided by the Word of God, you cannot fail to find God's best for your life. He gives you the spirit of wisdom and revelation so that you will be enlightened to understand the walk of righteousness.

My heart's cry before the Lord for you is that you will follow the Lord so closely that you will be rewarded for a life sold out to God. When the Lord comes back for us and we meet Him in the air, whatever your spiritual condition is right then is frozen in time, and you will be rewarded at the judgment seat of Christ for the deeds and works done here. You will be no closer to Jesus throughout eternity than you are the instant He returns.

May your heart's desire be to please the Lord. You are the children of the Light and children of the Day. The Lord has chosen you to be vessels of honor. May you be clothed with His radiant glory. In Jesus Name.

JESUS IS COMING SOON

May there be a steady flow of the Lord's blessings in your life. God is on the move to draw you ever closer to Him. He loves you with an all-encompassing love. His love will dispel and root out all darkness for He desires to fill you with Light. Jesus is the Light of the world. You are never alone. God is forever with you. He has the power to send angels to minister to you at any time. The Lord will always interact with you because He died to save you.

"Sanctify them through thy truth: thy word is truth." John 17:17

There was a couple traveling in Vancouver, Canada awhile back. They saw a nice looking hitchhiker and stopped to give him a ride. They talked for a few minutes and then the man said, "Jesus is coming soon. Prepare to meet Him, for it will not be long before He returns." The driver looked in her rear-view mirror and couldn't see him. She turned around but he wasn't there. She was swerving back and forth as she was looking for him and a cop stopped her and asked why she was driving all over the road. She told him about the man and what he had said but that he had disappeared and she was looking for him. The cop said, "You are the seventh person that I have stopped and they all have said the same thing.

May you be forever touched with heart-felt awesome blessings from the Lord. In Jesus Name.

GREATER WORKS

"Verily, verily, I saw unto you, He that believeth on me, the works that I do shall he do also; and greater works than these shall he do; because I go unto my Father. And whatsoever ye shall ask in my name, that will I do, that the Father may be glorified in the Son. If ye shall ask anything in my name, I will do it." John 14:12-14

How wonderful it is that we can follow in the steps of Jesus and do the works that He did, even greater works. This is accompanied with a dedicated life where no sin can block the answer to your prayers. Anything you read in your Bible about Jesus, you can ask him to multiply it. You can live like Jesus lived and do the works that Jesus did. This is a powerful promise of a power-packed life. If you lack wisdom, ask the Lord and He will give it to you. If you need to be stronger spiritually, ask the Lord and He will guide you into more truth. May you purpose in your heart to follow the Lord. He is your rock to stand on that steadies the course. He is your protector. The closer you get to Jesus, the greater He becomes. He is actually everything you will ever need.

May you be blessed in the most profound ways as you give yourself to the Lord and yield and obey His word. In Jesus Name.

GROW IN CHRIST

The walk of a Christian goes from glory to glory. Today you are at one spiritual level and as you grow in the grace and knowledge of the Lord, you grow to a higher level of spiritual maturity. The central purpose in life is to become more and more like Jesus. You take on His identity. Your understanding is enlightened to grasp the meaning of the more advanced teaching of the Word of God.

May His ultimate purpose be accomplished in your life today as you desire more of Him and He draws you closer with the blessings of goodness. From the day of your salvation, all sins were forgiven and you became a new creation in Christ. Old things were done away with and then all things became new. The Lord put away sin on the cross so that today sin should not be present in your life. You are cleansed by the blood of Jesus.

"Let us draw near with a true heart in full assurance of faith, having our hearts sprinkled from an evil conscience, and our bodies washed with pure water. Let us hold fast the profession of our faith without wavering; (for He is faithful that promised;) And let us consider one another to provoke unto love and to good works." Hebrews 10:22-23

Let us look at this thought. The Lord forgives sin when we repent, and He also "sprinkles" hearts from an evil conscience. No guilt.

May you willingly give the Lord your best and reap the eternal benefit and blessing of living free and unbound. He will multiply the good - ten, forty, sixty, a hundredfold. Never forget that God is almighty. He is powerful over all. The Lord will fulfill all your petitions and He will hear you from His holy heaven with the saving strength of His right hand. The blessing is that He will raise you up and you will stand strong. In Jesus Name.

BE LIKE-MINDED

It is the Lord who is mighty and glorious and it is He who holds you in the hollow of His hands. He would have you to stir up the good gift of God, which is in you to equip you for your destiny. He has great things in store for you to stand tall and be a powerful, godly influence to all those with whom you associate. Hold high the standard of holiness in your life. That is the Christ in you.

Be like-minded with the Holy Spirit. Agree with the Lord when He says that He has called you with a holy calling, not according to works, but according to His own purpose and grace, which was given you in Christ Jesus before the world began. My heart yearns for you to give your all to Jesus and let Him have His perfect will to further His kingdom on the earth through you.

"Let no man despise thy youth; but be thou an example of the believers, in word, in conversation, in charity, in spirit, in faith, in purity. Till I come, give attendance to reading, to exhortation, to doctrine. Neglect not the gift that is in thee." I Timothy 4:12-14

May the blessings of the Lord rest upon your mind, body, soul, heart and spirit. In Jesus Name.

IDLE WORDS

"But I say unto you, That every idle word that men shall speak, they shall give account thereof in the day of judgment. For by thy words thou shalt be justified, and by thy words thou shalt be condemned." Matthew 12:36-37

May you be blessed with a keen mind and a pure heart so that your words will be pleasing to the Lord. You will be blessed with clean thoughts of the diligent that tend only to plenteousness.

Idle words seem like a very small thing for the Lord to deem important but they are so important that He says He hears every word and also remembers them. He also knows your thoughts. When we all stand before the judgment seat of Christ, we will have to give an account for them and Jesus will judge whether the idle words and thoughts were good or bad.

God is interested in the small things you do, small acts of kindness, small acts of love, even giving a cup of cold water is giving consideration to the little things. Nothing is so small that the Lord does not take notice of it.

The Bible says that if we judge ourselves, we shall not be judged. We are to simply pray a prayer of repentance, asking forgiveness for the small things, then God forgives and you will not be judged later for the idle words and thoughts whether good or bad.

There is a holy work going on in all that pertains to your life. Though you may not be aware of all that God is doing, yet He is personally involved in bringing you into your destiny. His plans and purposes will not be stopped or thwarted by any circumstance or diversion. He will guide you into all truth and you will be led into all that He has promised.

You are so blessed, so loved, so purposely directed by the Lord that it will change your life as you become everything God wants you to be. God's blessing of purpose are upon you. In Jesus Name.

BLESSINGS OF GRACE

"Grace be to you, and peace, from God our Father, and from the Lord Jesus Christ." Ephesians 1:2

"But God, who is rich in mercy, for His great love wherewith He loved us, Even when we were dead in sins hath quickened us together with Christ, (by grace ye are saved;) And hath raised us up together, and made us sit together in heavenly places in Christ Jesus; That in the ages to come He might show the exceeding riches of His grace in His kindness toward us through Christ Jesus." Ephesians 2:4-7

The Lord bless you with His special kindness that is beyond human comprehension. You are blessed in His love that always radiates through His every action toward you. The deeper you live in His wonderful provisions, the deeper you realize just how great and excellent are the blessings of His love and grace that reaches out to you every day. You have a mighty God who is always there to bless you with great blessings. You are so loved.
In Jesus Name.

ABUNDANT LIFE

The Lord is high above the earth and His power is sufficient to bless you in ways you never thought possible. The grace of God over you is His tenderness and pure love that reaches everything about you. His love overshadows you and brings all things under His loving care. You receive great blessings when you yield to Him. Let Him have His way with you. He wants to personally bless you with a precious gift. He has wonderful things in store for you to bring you into a more radiant and fulfilling life.

"They shall see the glory of the Lord, and the excellency of our God." Isaiah 35:2

Be abundantly and marvelously blessed day and night. May the Lord's blessings go before you and come from behind and follow you and be on your right side and on your left. In Jesus Name.

GATES OF RIGHTEOUSNESS

There are many gates through which you will walk. God is always there to direct you in the right direction so that the gate you choose to walk through will be the right one. Little attention is given to your feet, so we now speak God's blessings over your feet so that He will guide your feet into the way of peace. Your feet will never go where there is riotous living, nor will they go where darkness resides. God will not allow your feet to be moved away from His chosen holy walk of blessing.

"Open to me the gates of righteousness: I will go into them, and I will praise the Lord: this gate of the Lord into which the righteous shall enter. I will praise thee: for thou hast heard me, and art become my salvation." Psalm 118:19-21

The gate of the Lord is carefully chosen for you by Him. Follow His direction and be gloriously blessed. You are always led in triumph. You feet shall always stand on the land that is blessed. The Lord shall preserve your going out and coming in from this time forth, and even forevermore. In Jesus Name.

LOVE

You are blessed with love. The most powerful force in the world is love. It overrules all other emotions and feelings. Love is tender and kind. Love is thoughtful of others. When love is in your heart, there is a softness and gentleness. The touch of love is noticeable. Love gives. Love reaches out and welcomes others to come in. You can feel when someone loves you. Love cares. Love is sustained by the Lord. It is nurtured and developed by the Lord. Love is taught by the Lord. It is not premeditated; it is spontaneous. Where love is absent, the Lord is absent. The motivation of good deeds is love, and it is love that God notices and thus rewards you with abundant blessings.

"Though I speak with the tongues of men and of angels, and have not charity, I am become as sounding brass, or a tinkling cymbal. And though I have the gift of prophecy, and understand all mysteries, and all knowledge; and though I have all faith, so that I could remove mountains, and have not charity, I am nothing.

"Love never fails." I Corinthians 13:1, 2, 8

May the blessings of the love of the Lord hold you near to Him and minister to your deepest need and restore all, redeem all, resurrect all, and conquer all things, that He have been given to you from the day you were born. In Jesus Name.

WORTHINESS

You are vital to God and were born to be blessed. He saw you from the womb and fashioned you to be His special one-of-a-kind individual. No one can fill your place with the Lord. You are very unique. You were made by the loving hands of God. There is never a day that He does not look upon you with tenderness to guide you into His perfect destiny for your life. He sometimes holds you in His lap just to love you. His Holy Spirit is sent to comfort you. You are his special creation.

All He asks of you is to keep the high standard of loving Him day in and day out, and place Him first in your life.

"Hereby know we that we dwell in Him, and He in us, because He hath given us of His Spirit.
"And we have seen and do testify that the Father sent the Son to be the Savior of the world.
"Whosoever shall confess that Jesus is the Son of God, God dwelleth in him and he in God.
"And we have known and believed the love that God hath to us. God is love; and he that dwelleth in love dwells in God, and God in him."
I John 4:13-16

May the Lord give you revelation of who you are in Him and blesses you with His peace and righteousness and marvelous grace. In Jesus Name.

ALL-SUFFICIENT GOD

Whenever there is competition for a time, be assured that when you put your relationship to God first, there are rewards of blessing that will follow you.

"For I know the thoughts that I think toward you, saith the Lord, thoughts of peace. and not of evil, to give you an expected end. Then shall ye call upon Me, and ye shall go and pray unto Me, and I will hearken unto you. And ye shall seek Me, and find Me, when ye shall search for Me with all your heart." Jeremiah 29:11-13

"For I will restore health unto you, and I will heal thee of thy wounds, saith the Lord." Jeremiah 30:17

The Lord is all-sufficient. There is nothing you want or need that He cannot provide. Some of what you may want will not further the cause of you walking closer to Him. His choice for you is always to step higher, leaning more on Him. He is there to bless you - always - in every circumstance, whether great or small. He works everything out for your good.

May you be abundantly blessed. May the Lord bless your soul with His joy, peace and contentment as you become more like Him. In Jesus Name.

STRONG FAITH

There is something about having faith in the Lord that is very stabilizing. It is a blessing when you believe God. You do not doubt because you put your trust in the unfailing Father. You are assured in your heart by the Holy Spirit that when you believe by faith for what is in your heart, He will do it. Sometimes you have to press in prayer to obtain your promise, but keep on believing. Touch the hem of His garment for your miracle, like the little woman in Luke 8:43-48. Jesus said to her, "Daughter, be of good comfort: thy faith has made thee whole: go in peace."

"So then faith cometh by hearing, and hearing by the Word of God." Romans 10:17

"Now the just shall live by faith." Hebrews 10:38

"But without faith it is impossible to please Him: for he that cometh to God must believe that He is, and that He is a rewarder of them that diligently seek Him." Hebrews 11:6

You are blessed with answered prayer and a hundredfold return of all you are believing God for. You are blessed with confidence, assurance, strength in your inner man, and are raised up to full stature to be all that God has called you to be. In Jesus Name.

SPIRITUALLY SOUND

"Let brotherly love continue. Be not forgetful to entertain strangers: for thereby some have entertained angels unawares." Hebrews13:1, 2

Did you realize that one of the strangers you met could possibly have been an angel? Give the Lord your excellent service.

May you not seek spiritual retirement, but rather join a Bible study or prayer meeting with a group who honors and loves God. Let love abound from your heart toward others. May you let every act be in love, and God will reward you with love from others.

May you consider the Lord the most incredible force in your life

and receive His bountiful blessings with thanksgiving. When something grieves you or causes confusion or negative thoughts, do not go there. Keep your mind clear and uncluttered between you and the Lord.

"But thanks be to God, which giveth us the victory through our Lord Jesus Christ.

Therefore, my beloved brethren, be ye steadfast, unmovable, always abounding in the work of the Lord, forasmuch as ye know that your labor is not in vain in the Lord." I Corinthians 15:57, 58

May you be blessed with the loving favor of God. May the blessing of excellence follow you in all your ways. May you rise up and refuse the lowlands of the world. May you be blessed more and more as you walk in a spirit of oneness with your God. In Jesus Name.

AFFIRMATION

"His lord said unto him, Well done, thou good and faithful servant: thou hast been faithful over a few things; I will make thee ruler over many things: enter thou into the joy of thy Lord." Matthew 25:21

The greatest blessing after a day's work, is to hear the Lord say, "Well done, my good and faithful servant." This affirmation from Jesus brings sweet peace to your soul, and is the coveted response every believer desires when they one day see Jesus face to face.

Each night, it is good to think over your day and praise the Lord for the blessings, repent where you could have done better, and yield yourself to God to refine you to be more and more like Jesus. The Lord has equipped you with many good gifts that are to be used for His purposes. He is aware when you are faithful over the few things. And tomorrow He will broaden your field of service to be ruler over the many things. What He then invites you to do is to enter into the joy of the Lord. Joy means cheerfulness, calm delight, and exceedingly joyful.

"The joy of the Lord is your strength." Nehemiah 8:10

How great and marvelous are God's promises to you. His wonderful blessings overshadow your very life day in and day out. You are blessed to maintain mental poise which is established on the truth that God is holy love. In Jesus Name.

ETERNAL LIFE

Our lives are eternal. From birth forward, our lives will never end. We will spend our time here on earth preparing for an endless life in eternity. God has given us twenty-four hours a day to become more and more like Jesus. It is a process of yielding our wills to God's will. You are blessed and chosen by God to fulfill His divine purpose. He has given you gifts and callings that enable you to be transformed into His likeness.

"And be not conformed to this world: but be ye transformed by the renewing of your mind, that ye may prove what is that good, and acceptable, and perfect, will of God." Romans 12:2

You are blessed with a freedom to live for Christ in this life. This blessing frees you from the bondage of sin and a distorted past. Faith in the name of Jesus and the cross gives you an inheritance to live forever in heaven with Jesus, God, the Holy Spirit and myriads of angels, and all the righteous departed saints. You are blessed to one day live throughout eternity with all the saints mentioned in your Bible. This glorious hope is the ultimate blessing. In Jesus Name.

BODY OF CHRIST

All believers in the world makes up a harmonious blending of different streams of thought and characteristics of life, yet so perfectly blended to make up the body of Christ. Each has his own calling, yet the whole body moves in synch with other parts. Every member is beloved of the Lord. You are blessed, redeemed, restored and made whole for you are in the body of Christ. You always carry Jesus in your heart wherever you go.

"But now hath God set the members every one of them in the body, as it hath pleased Him. That there should be no schism in the body; but that the members should have the same care one for another. And whether one member suffer, all the members suffer with it, or one member be honored, all the members rejoice with it. Now ye are the body of Christ, and members in particular." I Corinthians 12:18, 25-27

Because we are all connected, may you increase in spiritual strength to be a blessing to this body of believers by holding up the hands of weaker members in prayer, standing strong in the ministry where God has called you. May Christ be magnified in your body with strength and fortitude. In Jesus Name.

HOLY SPIRIT LEADS

You are blessed with the will to adjust your life to the will of God so that He can do the ultimate for you. You are promised greatness for you are a child of God, and there is nothing small or insignificant with Him. He saved you to bring you into your destiny that He wants to fulfill so that you can rise to the level He wants you to take. You will keep soaring higher as you listen to the Lord and obey what He says. He will never tell you to do anything that He has not equipped you for and is not written in your Bible.

He is a holy God and He will lead you in holiness. You will daily grow in the strength and wisdom and understanding of the Lord. Your strength in God will turn your eyes from the unprofitable things of the world and you will have no desire to follow foolish people.

"God raiseth up the poor out of the dust, and lifteth the needy out of the dunghill; that He may set him with princes, even with the princes of His people." Psalm 113:7, 8

You are blessed by this promise in the Word of God that your future is to be seated with princes. You will be filled with His Holy Spirit who will fill your heart and soul with peace and hope. Be encouraged. God is for you so who can be against you. In Jesus Name.

VOICE OF THE LORD

"The voice of the Lord is powerful; the voice of the Lord is full of majesty. The Lord will give strength unto His people; the Lord will give strength unto His people; the Lord will bless His people with peace." Psalm 29:4, 11

All heaven responds to the voice of the Lord. When He speaks, everyone in heaven reacts. God's voice is the most powerful voice in the world. And every word in the Bible is God's voice speaking to you. It is the living Word. Faith activates the Word. Your Bible is filled with promises that you can stand on and they are activated by your faith. Every promise was spoken to give you hope and life.

"For whatsoever is born of God overcometh the world; and this is the victory that overcometh the world, even our faith." I John 5:4

Believe God. There is a constant assurance in the Lord and that is what you want to depend upon. In times like these, you cannot trust worldly systems or people, but you can always trust Jesus. You belong to Him and when you go to Him, He is always there for you. Purpose in your heart to live by faith in Jesus. Be strong in faith and victory will come.

The Lord will guide you, give you ample provision for all your needs, and you will be blessed to see just how strong He is in your life. He is a powerful God. You will never lose when you put your trust in Him. This is the confidence that you have in Him, that, if you ask anything according to His will, he hears you, and if He hears you, whatsoever you ask, you know that you have the petitions that you desired of Him. Rejoice and praise the Lord for you are abundantly blessed. In Jesus Name.

TENDER HEARTS

Holiness is declared over your lives.

Oh Lord, part the heavens with Your voice.

Open their ears to hear what You are saying to them.

Lord, give them tender hearts and soft spirits like that of Jesus.

Send the peace that is in heaven to surround their lives.

Tenderly and lovingly hold them in Your arms and breathe new life into their souls and spirits.

Reveal to them the blessings that come when they respect and obey You.

Purpose to keep your hands clean and your hearts pure by going to God in prayer for help.

"But let all those that put their trust in the Lord rejoice; let them ever shout for joy, because thou defendest them; let them also that love thy name be joyful in thee.

For thou, Lord, wilt bless the righteous; with favor wilt thou compass him as with a shield." Psalm 5:11, 12

Be marvelously blessed with freedom and joy of the Lord. In Jesus Name.

POWERFUL BLESSINGS

You are so blessed to have Jesus in your heart. The Savior who came down from heaven and became a man so that He could bear the sins of the entire world by dying on a cross and shedding His blood that cleanses us from sin, and came out of the grave and now sits at the right hand of God. The blessing of the power of the blood unlocks souls out of a worldly mindset and transfers all thoughts, words, actions, desires and habits onto Jesus who gives you the mind of Christ. Just one dynamic experience with Jesus where He saved your soul and you suddenly exchange a life of sin and death to receive resurrection life with unending blessings. Thank you, Jesus, for your unfathomable love.

"And there came a voice from heaven saying, Thou art my beloved son, in whom I am well pleased." Mark 1:11

You were born to receive the blessings God has for you. There are many piled around Jesus and He is waiting for you to ask Him from a heart of love and dedication to bless you. You will receive them and will not live another day walking in the ways of the world and being robbed of God's unlimited blessings. You are destined for the throne in heaven where you will rule and reign with Jesus throughout eternity. In Jesus Name.

IT IS TIME

"And it shall come to pass afterward, that I will pour out My Spirit upon all flesh; and your sons and your daughters shall prophesy, your old men shall dream dreams, your young men shall see visions: And also upon the servants and upon the handmaids in those days will I pour out My Spirit." Joel 2:28-29

The day is here that the Lord is doing mighty works in the land. His hand is reaching out to use anyone who will make themselves available to Him. One touch of the Lord's favor on those who believe and an explosive blessing follows. He is not playing around with half-hearted Christians anymore. He is returning to the earth for us very soon and until then, those who are truly connected to God, will be blessed beyond their highest expectations.

Mighty is the hand of the Lord upon your life. He has never left you nor forsaken you. You have become everything God has wanted you to be to reach your destiny. You are filled with His excellence and integrity. He has worked all that into your character. Now you are ready for Him to bend heaven to fulfill His purposes in your life. Yield and obey and see the manifold blessings He will pour upon you. In Jesus Name.

RUN WITH A VISION

"Beloved, if God so loved us, we ought also to love one another. No man hath seen God at any time. If we love one another, God dwelleth in us, and His love is perfected in us.
Hereby know we that we dwell in Him, and He in us, because He hath given us of His Spirit. And we have seen and do testify that the Father sent the Son to be the Savior of the world." I John 4:11-14

This is one powerful scripture! It confirms you lack nothing. God says you are loved. If you love one another, God dwells in you. His love is perfected in you. You remain in God. God remains in you. His Holy Spirit remains in you.

You are there, right now, today, and you are everything God wants you to be. Let your mind grasp just how limitless you are when you walk with God. He will open doors of opportunity for you to fulfill your destiny that you never thought possible. He is the God of the overflow and He will carry you through to unbelievable accomplishments. Believe God and be abundantly blessed.
In Jesus Name.

SIN WEAKENS

May you not yield to any worldly temptation or desire that would block or hinder God's promised blessings in your life. The Lord will give you everything you need. It will all come from Him and you will have peace of mind. You will find that your walk is to be blessed with new vision and more freedom in God to do what will fit easily in the higher walk of blessing.

"Blessed is the man that trusteth in the Lord, and whose hope the Lord is." Jeremiah 17:7

The Lord is your rock and confidence who keeps you safe and protected. May you be blessed in your homes, blessed in your jobs, blessed in all your relationships, blessed in your daily activities, blessed in your relationship with the Lord, blessed with an intelligent mind, blessed with a healthy body, blessed in all your choices, blessed with godly wisdom, blessed with joy and happiness, and blessed of the Lord to fulfill His perfect destiny that He has planned for your life. In Jesus Name.

AIM IN LIFE

Take time to be thankful, for there is power for blessing in thanksgiving. Stir up your gratitude by remembering what the Lord has done for you. In so doing you will enter the realm of His presence and stand in holiness before His throne. There is nothing more pure in the kingdom than a grateful heart. Bring your perfect sacrifice of praise and be blessed. Praise and worship locks out the powers of darkness. Lifting up the name of the Lord in thanksgiving blocks all the power of the enemy.

"Enter into His gates with thanksgiving, and into His courts with praise. Be thankful unto Him, and bless His name." Psalms 100:4

"The Lord hath been mindful of us: He will bless us: the house of Israel; he will bless the house of Aaron. He will bless them that fear the Lord, both small and great. The Lord shall increase you more and more, you and your children. Ye are blessed of the Lord which made heaven and earth." Psalm 115:12-15

May the Lord lift you to a new realm of honoring Him, as you receive all the wonderful blessings that will come on you with love and thankfulness to Him. He is good and his mercy is everlasting and His truth endures to all generations. Truth encompasses security, fidelity, faithfulness, stability, steadiness, all of which the Lord blesses you with. In Jesus Name.

COME UP

"Mercy unto you, and peace, and love, be multiplied." Jude 2

The Lord is calling you to come up in the Holy Spirit into the heavenly realm, this place where wisdom, knowledge and understanding is boundless and where the secrets of your holy God are revealed. Come to this place each and every day where the door is always open for you to meet with the Lord, just you and Him. May you answer the call to seek the Lord. He will do for you more than you ever expected.

"Submit yourselves therefore to God. Resist the devil and he will flee from you." James 4:7

"Behold, I stand at the door, and knock; if any man hear my voice, and open the door, I will come in to him, and will sup with him, and he with Me." Revelation 3:20

The Lord has blessed you with holy boldness to stretch out and take hold of His hand. May you let God come into your heart in a deeper way. Great peace will come as you yield to Him and you begin to see breakthroughs that were never thought possible. In Jesus Name.

SUPERNATURAL SENSE

"For thou art a holy people unto the Lord thy God: the Lord thy God has chosen you to be a special people unto Himself, above all people that are upon the face of the earth." Deuteronomy 7:6

May the blessing of the Lord be upon every area of your life that has failed to be productive. May His blessings open great opportunities to walk in the fullness of the destiny that He has for you. May you feel God's love come around you and in every part of your mind, heart, body, soul and spirit. May His blessings revive your spirit. May He lead you in a way of righteousness that you may inherit His enlightening promises.

"The blessing of the Lord, it maketh rich, and He addeth no sorrow with it." Proverbs 10:22

"Thou art the God that doest wonders: thou hast declared thy strength among the people." Psalm 77:14

My father, raise up all these people to yield their lives to You so that they be used in glorious ways to bring glory to the name of the Lord. We declare holiness, righteousness, goodness and sinless living over them that the life of Christ be manifested through them every day. In Jesus Name.

BLOOD OF JESUS IS POWER

Behind every negative attitude there is an unresolved story that we must deal with at God's throne of grace, if we are to attain overcoming victory and enjoy His peace.

This is the Word of the Lord saying, "Not by might, nor by power, but by My Spirit, saith the Lord of Hosts." Zechariah 4:6

Through the Blood of Jesus that was shed on the cross when He gave His life that all mankind might accept Him as Savior, is the most powerful weapon used against the forces of darkness.

When you believed in your heart that Jesus died for your sins to be forgiven, it was the blood of Christ that cleansed you and washed away all your sins, past, present and future. The Blood of Jesus is life-giving. It is eternal.

The Blood of Jesus is your witness and the word of your testimony. The Blood of Jesus is speaking that you are an overcomer. Through the Blood you have complete victory over all sin of every description. Mankind has never committed a sin too heinous and godless that the Blood of Jesus cannot cleanse. Whosoever calls upon the name of Jesus shall be saved.

The Blood of Jesus is speaking that you are justified and made righteous. May you declare that you are now innocent and not guilty, because you have asked forgiveness and confessed your sins and shortcomings to Jesus. The Blood of Jesus cleanses you from all unrighteousness.

The Blood of Jesus declares that you are redeemed, set free and delivered from every disease and infirmity, and you walk in perfect health that Jesus paid for on the cross by the stripes He bore on His back.

The Blood of Jesus strengthens, completes, perfects and makes you what you were created for by equipping you with gifts and fruits of the Holy Spirit so that you may carry out God's will. God is working in you by His Spirit, accomplishing that which is pleasing in His sight through Jesus.

Be abundantly blessed by the pure pleasure of God who wants to fill you to overflow with His goodness. In Jesus Name.

FRAGMENTS

"When they were filled, He said unto his disciples, Gather up the fragments that remain, that nothing be lost. Therefore they gathered them together, and filled twelve baskets with the fragments of the five barley loaves which remained over and above unto them that had eaten." John 6:12, 13

God takes all the fragments of your life and fills baskets full with these fragments. He takes everything that has ever happened to you, all the broken pieces, all the good and the bad, and gathers them up that nothing be lost. He has saved them for Him to use to be a light of encouragement and strength to a darkened world that needs to hear and be delivered from their life of sin.

God will use the testimony of your life to give hope to multitudes. Nothing is ever wasted. Nothing was ever meant to be forgotten and not used in the future. The Lord blesses each and every piece of all you have ever experienced and then puts His blessings upon you as He uses you to take from your twelve baskets to bless others.

It has always been God's intention to bring you out of all that has kept you bound so He could powerfully use you to bless the multitudes who are hungry and need a Savior. In Jesus Name.

FOLLOW ME, BUT FIRST

"And Jesus said unto him, Follow Me.
And then he said to another, Follow Me."
And they said to Him,
But first . . . ."
Luke 9:59-62

But first - one said he had to bury his father before he could follow Jesus.
But first - said the other I will follow you but let me bid farewell to those at home at my house.

Jesus' reply to the first was, "Let the dead bury the dead, but go thou and preach the kingdom of God."

Jesus' reply to the other was, "No man, having put his hand to the plough, and looking back, is fit for the kingdom of God."

How many times has the Lord said, "Follow Me," and the reply has been, "Okay - but first . . . ." and we do what we think is more important before answering the call to "Follow Me"?

Many blessings have been forfeited because something else was more important to us than Jesus. Also, how many souls will never make it to heaven because we were unwilling to go when Jesus called. To follow Jesus and obey His voice when you hear Him calling, is the most important decision and choice you will ever make. May your answer be, "Yes, Lord. I will follow You."

May you be blessed with a tender heart toward Him and enter into the joy of the Lord, so that you reap a hundredfold for your obedience to Him. May His love cover you and you love Him with all your heart, soul, mind and strength.
In Jesus Name.

HOLY SERVANT

God has established you in dignity, like angels in holiness, and appointed you to proclaim His Word by your life and teaching. Your protection from sin is living a holy life. The reason holy living is so profound is that the blood of Jesus has cleansed you from all evil and worldliness that would muddy your life. Your mind is clear, your conscience is free of guilt, and your heart is pure. That allows you to have blessings that touch everything that concerns you. Always remember, sin is a worthless experience.

"But as He which hath called you is holy, so be ye holy in all manner of conversation;
Because it is written, be ye holy; for I am holy." I Peter 1:15, 16

"Seeing ye have purified your souls in obeying the truth through the Spirit unto unfeigned love of the brethren, see that ye love one another with a pure heart fervently." I Peter 1:22

"Humble yourselves therefore under the mighty hand of God, that He may exalt you in due time. Casting all your care upon Him; for He careth for you." I Peter 5:6, 7

May the Lord bless your life with His presence and establish, strengthen and settle you, making you a powerful servant of the Most High God. In Jesus Name.

CUP OF COLD WATER

"For whosoever shall give you a cup of water to drink in My name, because ye belong to Christ, verily I say unto you, he shall not lose his reward." Mark 9:41

"And whosoever shall give to drink unto one of these little ones a cup of cold water only in the name of a disciple, verily I say unto you, he shall in no wise lose his reward." Matthew 10:42

One day, I was at my youngest daughter's home and mentioned that I was thirsty, and in just a minute, Hannah, my six-year old granddaughter, walked up to me and handed me a cup of cold water with ice in it. I was not aware that she had heard me say I was thirsty. It was such a small gesture, but it touched my heart because the Lord spoke to me that even a cup of cold water is noticed by the Lord - even to the extent that when you give a cup of water, you will be rewarded. Likewise, giving a cup of water to a little child is noticed by the Lord and rewarded for your kindness and thoughtfulness and caring attitude.

"Whether therefore ye eat, or drink, or whatsoever ye do, do all to the glory of God." I Corinthians 10:31

May you be blessed with wisdom, knowledge, faith, love, and walk quietly and with great assurance with the Lord your God. In Jesus Name.

UNFLINCHING LOYALTY

"The Lord shall command the blessing upon thee in thy storehouses, and in all that thou settest thine hand unto; and He shall bless thee in the land which the Lord thy God giveth thee. And the Lord shall make thee the head, and not the tail; and thou shallt be above only, and thou shalt not be beneath; if that thou hearken to the commandments of the Lord thy God, which I command thee this day, to observe and to do them." Deuteronomy 28: 8, 13

"The righteous also shall hold on his way, and he that hath clean hands shall be stronger and stronger." Job 17:9

Remain true to God and He will move heaven and hell for you. That is blessing. To sincerely have the mindset to please the Lord with all your actions, words and thoughts is quite uncommon in today's world. Very few really desire to walk close to Jesus. But for those who love Him, they are the ones who will experience all the joys and fulfillment of His abundant life that He has promised them.

My three children were given a heart of unflinching loyalty to God first, and to me as their mother. They have a depth of character and wisdom that is rarely found. The soundness and faithfulness of their love has always been very unique and powerful. They are a wonderful inspiration. I love them with all my heart, soul and spirit forever. Mightily bless them, Lord, in every way.

May He bless you with harmony and favor among all your friends and family. You shall experience utmost blessings from His mighty hand. You are one of those that He has chosen to walk the closest to Him. In Jesus Name.

ARISE AND SHINE

"Blessed be the God and Father of our Lord Jesus Christ, who hath blessed us with all spiritual blessings in heavenly places in Christ." Ephesians 1:3

You are truly blessed with all spiritual blessings and gifts to arise and take your place in God, as servants of Christ, doing the will of God from your heart. He calls you to forget those things which are behind, and reaching forth unto those things which are before you, and press toward the mark for the prize of the high calling of God in Christ Jesus, that your destiny may be fulfilled with purpose. You are no longer withheld, you are no longer restricted, you are no longer living under the darkness of that which satan brought into your life for the moment. God gives you life as you overcome that which wars against you.

In Christ there is hope, which is to anticipate with pleasure, expectation and confidence. Christ in you is your hope of glory. You want to walk in such a way that pleases God, so that you will abound and super-abound more and more. You are blessed with encouragement from the Holy Spirit because all things are working for your good to promote you.

Now turn and face the glory of God. In Jesus Name.

YOU ARE WORTHY

You always have access into the presence of the Lord by the Holy Spirit. You cannot ask anything that is too big for God. He is over the top. Just believe by faith in the Lord that you will walk in newness of life without an evil conscience of feeling guilty or unworthy to come before Him. Exercise faith to believe God that you are in His presence constantly. Have faith in the power of God and the blood of Jesus to cleanse anything in your life that would stand between Him and you.

"How much more shall the blood of Christ, who through the eternal Spirit offered Himself without spot to God, purge your conscience from dead works to serve the living God?" Hebrews 9:14

You do not have to do anything to help God like you. He sees you through Christ. Your relationship to God is open and free and motivated by the Spirit of God. You have favor by the blood of Jesus. You have daily blessings by the Holy Spirit of God. You are in a season of His supernatural grace, His unlimited favor of having all kinds of empowering gifts from the Holy Spirit. You never need to perform for God to like you or favor you. Just run to the blood of Jesus that covers you and makes you whole. His mercies are new every morning.

You are abundantly blessed - every minute of every day. This is God's favor to you. You have been chosen by the mighty God of the universe. In Jesus Name.

QUIETNESS

"For as many as are led by the Spirit of God, they are the sons of God." Romans 8:14

You are blessed to walk under the Spirit of grace and have a free and easy style that is so natural. It will almost seem as though you have not acted at all. When your spirit is centered on God, all activity He initiates will be noble, full of peace, natural, and so spontaneous that it will appear to you there has hardly been any activity at all. The Lord has moved through you and given you His personality and His character.

"But to be spiritually minded is life and peace." Romans 8:6

You are carrying the Holy Spirit's anointing. This is something you will want to protect and never be shameful by any discolored action. This is the Christ in you and has nothing to do with pride. When you have that anointing, you will walk very circumspectly so as not to quench the Holy Spirit.

This is the walk that honors the holiness and presence of the Holy Spirit. You will never know it is on you. God will not let you know. He protects it. So you walk undisturbed by earthly things for your confidence and security is set in the Lord. In Jesus Name.

PRAY THE WORD

"The Lord is gracious, and full of compassion; slow to anger, and of great mercy.
The Lord is good to all; and His tender mercies are over all His works." Psalm 145:8-9

"The Lord upholdeth all that fall, and raiseth up all those that be bowed down.
The eyes of all wait upon thee; and thou givest them their meat in due season.
Thou openest thine hand, and satisfiest the desire of every living thing.
The Lord is righteous in all His ways, and holy in all His works.
The Lord is nigh unto all them that call upon Him, to all that call upon Him in truth.
He will fulfill the desire of them that fear Him: He also will hear their cry, and will save them. The Lord preserveth all them that love Him." Psalm 145: 14-20

When you read every line of this scripture and take it to heart by standing in faith that it was spoken directly to you, it will be surprising how your life will change. This word will stir your spirit when it is mixed with faith. Pray this scripture. Lift it up to the Lord and claim these promises.

May the Lord be very tender with you and may He show His complete compassion for you in every area of your life. His eyes are on the smallest sparrow and His eyes are surely upon you. What is your need? What would you like God to work out for you? Just talk to Him. Tell Him all that is on your heart. He will listen to every word. You will have His full attention. And when you have opened up your heart to Him, He will kindly reach down and touch your very soul and will work out all things according to the counsel of His own will and you will be abundantly blessed. In Jesus Name.

PRAY NOW

The Lord is righteous and holy and desires His people to be like Him. Having a personal relationship with Jesus as the Lord of your life gives strength to your inner spirit like none else. As you talk to the Lord who is God of the Universe, who is over all things, sees all things, knows the end from the beginning, and has a distinct plan for your life, all of this coupled together sends this message, that God loves you with a heavenly love that supersedes any earthly love.

God is for you and if God be for you who can be against you. Allow the Lord to move you to higher spiritual realms so He can bless you with all spiritual blessings in heavenly places in Christ.

Let hope arise in your heart and believe by faith that God is blessing you and is establishing you and bringing you into a more solid and secure walk with Him.

"Hear instruction, and be wise, and refuse it not. Blessed is the man that heareth me, watching daily at my gates, waiting at the posts of my doors. For whoso findeth me findeth life, and shall obtain favor of the Lord." Proverbs 8:33-35

May the Lord bless you with honesty, integrity and give you favor with all people, both friend and foe. May He pour out His mercy and grace, and give you wisdom and direct your steps. May you be . blessed with many loyal friends, and surrounded with people who love you. May you be blessed as God steps into every situation you are faced with and clears out the clutter and brings in His masterful peace that no one can rob from you. In Jesus Name.

HAND OF GOD

May you be raised to the highest level of ministry in the destiny that the Lord has called you to do. May His hand be forever upon you to anoint with His Holy Spirit. May the Lord bring you out of the old and into the new season of your life where there are new capabilities and possibilities. May all the debris and hindrances be wiped out by the power of the blood of Jesus. May you see new horizons that you never knew were there and walk in tremendous blessings. May all things bow under the mighty hand of God that do not agree with God's eternal purpose for your life.

You are mighty in God. His hand is upon you. You are destined to succeed in all that the Lord leads you to do. His ability is your ability. His favor is all over you. His love sustains you. His mighty presence walks with you.

"Blessings are upon the head of the just." Proverbs 10:6

"And they that know thy name will put their trust in thee: for thou, Lord, hast not forsaken them that seek thee." Psalm 9:10

"Touching the Almighty, we cannot find Him out: He is excellent in power, and in judgment, and in plenty of justice: He will not afflict." Job 37:23

You are blessed to hear and comprehend the deep truths of the Word of God. He will teach you at a level that you will become better acquainted with the God of the Bible. He will fill your heart with an eagerness to learn more so that you may give the truth to others. In Jesus Name.

RUN THE RACE

"Know ye not that they which run in a race run all, but one receiveth the prize? So run, that you may obtain.

"And every man that strives for the mastery is temperate in all things. Now they do it to obtain a corruptible crown, but we an incorruptible.

"I therefore so run, not as uncertainly; so fight I, not as one that beateth the air:

"But I keep under my body, and bring it into subjection: lest that by any means, when I have preached to others, I myself should be a castaway." I Corinthians 9:24-27

Paul, the great apostle, tells us how he passionately pursued the highest of goals – Christ-likeness. His goal was to win Christ as Bridegroom. To rule and reign with Christ throughout eternity was his reward for dedicated service. It is a word from the Lord that we are to be conformed into the very image of Christ.

Athletes endure severe training to go for the gold, with one important difference. For the athlete, the cheering crowds would soon vanish and all that is left is the cherished prize sitting on a table or hung on a wall. But not so with the prize Paul tells us to pursue. We go through the sometimes harsh training of life that develops character that we may become like Christ. And for this we receive the approval from the Lord, and from the heavenly cloud of witnesses who cheers us on.

May you be blessed as you run this Christian race to be like Christ. Your reward is great and throughout all eternity you will be forever blessed that you gave your all to win Christ as the bridegroom of your soul. The Lord bless you as you lead the life of an Overcomer. In Jesus Name.

NATURAL TALENT

All work done for the glory of God is noble and many of you were born with a natural talent that comes so easy for you.

"And whatsoever ye do in word or deed, do all in the name of the Lord Jesus, giving thanks to God, and the Father by Him." Colossians 3:17

"And whatsoever ye do, do it heartily as to the Lord, and not unto men: Knowing that of the Lord ye shall receive the reward of the inheritance: for ye serve the Lord Christ." Colossians 3:23-24

One of the joys in life is to know the gifting that God has given you, and do it to the glory of God. Each one of you have what is called a natural talent and when you do what you are naturally inclined to do, then the work gives you satisfaction and happiness and God honors you with prosperity. Imagination is turned to creativity. Pursue that to the glory of God and you will be successful - and happy.

"I wisdom dwell with prudence, and find out knowledge of witty inventions." Proverbs 8:12

May you be blessed with all spiritual blessings. May the Lord give you gifts that will make you prosperous. May He lift your spirit and fill you with joy and happiness. May you have favor all around you and find contentment, rest and peace. In Jesus Name.

RIGHTLY RELATED

Choose to live your life that overflows with praise and thanksgiving to the Lord. The Lord inhabits the praises of His people, meaning He dwells in the place where you are praising Him. It is good to keep your soul rightly related to God.

"O give thanks unto the Lord, for He is good: for His mercy endureth forever. Oh that men would praise the Lord for His goodness, and for His wonderful works to the children of men. For He satisfieth the longing soul, and filleth the hungry soul with goodness. Whoso is wise, and will observe these things, even they shall understand the loving-kindness of the Lord." Psalm 107:1, 8, 9, 43

May the Lord give you double blessings as you choose to follow and obey Him. May He fill your heart with gladness and contentment. May you be fully satisfied with the many things He has blessed you with. May He give you deep revelation of His love for you. May He restore to you the joy of His salvation; and uphold you with His free Spirit. Smile and watch how many people you will bless. Show love and you will receive love. Be abundantly blessed. In Jesus Name.

TO WIN YOU BACK

Nothing in your life is ever lost, for God restores all things back to you sevenfold. The Lord will continually use everything for your good. The work of Jesus in any person's life is always redemptive (to win you back).

"And we know that all things work together for good, to them that love God, to them who are the called according to His purpose." Romans 8:28

Somewhere in your life you had a dream and possibly your dream has yet to come true. But it will.

The Lord told Habakkuk in the Bible to:

"Write the vision, and make it plain upon tables, that he may run that readeth it.

For the vision is yet for an appointed time, but at the end it shall speak, and not lie: though it tarry, wait for it; for it will surely come; it will not tarry." Habakkuk 2:2-3

In other words, when God's timing is right, there is nothing that can stop it.

May there be such a presence of the Lord upon you and you are so blessed because He is about to move in your life in a remarkable way. You will be highly anointed and blessed for the Lord is preparing something wonderful for you. In Jesus Name.

GOD'S INNER WORK

It is more important what God does in you than what He does through you.

Because the quality of what He does through you will be determined by what He does in you.

Know God. Walk with God. Accomplish the will of God. These are three of the most important things you can do with your life.

Be aligned with Jesus. He has a master plan.

"Now the Lord is that Spirit: and where the Spirit of the Lord is, there is liberty:

But we all, with open face beholding as in a glass the glory of the Lord, are changed into the same image from glory to glory, even as by the Spirit of the Lord." II Corinthians 3:17-18

The Lord desires you to be changed into His likeness. He desires you to be like Him and have His glory on you. Maturity has many facets like a diamond. The more facets, the greater the brilliance.

May you be blessed with all spiritual blessings and you forever be drawn closer to the Lord that the light of Jesus shine brighter and brighter as you yield to Him. May He multiply His wonderful blessings upon your life. In all things manifest a drawing upon the grace of God that will make you a marvel to yourself and to others. Draw now. In Jesus Name.

SUPERNATURAL

God is a God of miracles. He does things on a daily basis that are supernatural. The natural is what anyone can do. Natural tendencies are man's abilities. But when the need is something beyond the mental, physical, natural talent, skill and aptitude that men have, then God steps in.

When you need something beyond your natural abilities, that is the call to pray and bring Him into the picture. And God does the supernatural in answer to your prayers. And He loves doing that for you. There is nothing too hard for the Lord. Absolutely nothing. Step out into the irresistible future with Jesus.

"The Lord is not slack concerning His promise, as some men count slackness; but is long-suffering to us-ward, not willing that any should perish, but that all should come to repentance." II Peter 3:9

The Spirit of the Lord God wants to reverse all the bad out and pull all the good and the normal back into your life. He wants to give you beauty for ashes, the oil of joy for mourning, the garment of praise for the spirit of heaviness; that you might be called trees (people) of righteousness, the planting of the Lord, that God might be glorified.

So be gloriously blessed, my precious family and readers. May the Lord send His ministering angels to surround you and all that pertains to you, that your heart may be encouraged and strengthened and full of hope and expectancy, for He is about to work miracles for you. In Jesus Name.

TOO SOON TO QUIT

The hands that were pierced move the wheels of human history and mold the circumstances of individual lives.

You are on Jesus' team.

The greatest success is in rising every time you fall.

The Israelis say that nothing is impossible. It just takes a little longer.

Think big. You have the mind of a big God.

No matter what the problems are, do not stop. Just do not give up. It is always too soon to quit.

The secret to lasting success is lasting.

Many times I have wanted to give up but I never really knew what I would do if I did.

"The Lord hath done great things for us; whereof we are glad." Psalm 126:3

"The Lord is good to all; and His tender mercies are over all His works." Psalm 145:9

May the powerful works of God make you fruitful. May He show up in your every circumstance showing Himself mighty. The Lord is over all and everything shall bow to His perfect will. Nothing goes unnoticed by the Lord if it pertains to you, for you are His chosen. You were bought with a price and His blood covers you with total protection and direction. God is for you and is leading you in the right direction. In Jesus Name.

ENTIRELY COMPLETE

Become the hand of God to those in need.

"Delight thyself also in the Lord, and He shall give thee the desires of thine heart." Psalm 37:4

What better qualifications could there be for future blessings than that you be perfect and entirely complete, wanting or lacking nothing.

God's express purpose for you is to bring good out of all your circumstances. He is looking at the end result. The measure of your life's success is not where you were when you started out, but where you are when you finish.

A few things in life are permanent - including success and failure.

As you trust in the Lord, sooner or later you will "connect" and many will be affected for good. Seek to make a good name for yourself in your character, words and deeds, and your standing with the Lord. This will be a tremendous blessing to you all of your life. God loves you. His highest joy is that the purpose of your life be fulfilled.

May you be abundantly blessed and may time be restored to you. All the time that has been wasted, God wants to restore it back to you. May He compact your life with effectiveness, allowing you to accomplish in months what used to take years, and enable you to accomplish in days what could have taken a lifetime.

"For with God, nothing shall be impossible." Luke 1:37

In Jesus Name.

CONTENTED LIFE

In the Bible, God set boundaries around those things He wanted protected.

He set pillars - piles of stones - veils - the Jordan River - doors - doorposts – thresholds - - gates. His boundaries were to keep the evil of the world out.

That which was outside of His gates was subject to the evil of the world.

That which was inside His gates was protected.

Jesus died on the cross and shed His blood to bring salvation to the world and it is that salvation that extends to every part of your life. When He asked the children of Israel to put the blood over the doorposts, it protected all those inside the house. In prayer, ask God to draw a line of the blood of Jesus as a boundary around your life and your home as protection from all that is in the world.

"How excellent is thy loving-kindness, O God! Therefore the children of men put their trust under the shadow of thy wings." Psalm 36:7

You are crowned with favor and goodness. May your life be fully contented and filled with explosive blessings. God rules right where you are. In Jesus Name.

HEAVENLY REWARD

"Eye hath not seen, nor ear heard, neither have entered into the heart of man, the things which God hath prepared for them that love Him." I Corinthians 2:9

You have a reward in heaven that is already prepared for those who love God.

"And behold, I come quickly; and my reward is with me, to give every man according as his work shall be. I am Alpha and Omega, the beginning and the end, the first and the last. Blessed are they that do His commandments, that they may have right to the tree of life, and may enter in through the gates into the city." Revelation 22:12-14

The description of a new heaven and a new earth is in Revelation 21. The first heaven and the first earth were passed away. And the nations of them which are saved shall walk in the light of it. And the city had no need of the sun, neither of the moon, to shine in it; for the glory of God did lighten it, and the Lamb is the light thereof.

The Apostle John, who was given the book of Revelation, was the first living person to see the new heaven and the new earth. He also saw the holy city, new Jerusalem, coming down from God out of heaven and the street of the city was pure gold, and each of the twelve foundations were each of precious stones.

This is what your heavenly reward will be and it makes all that you go through on earth worth the struggle for God shall surely reward you for all the good you have done. Likewise, each one will suffer loss if their works are burned up like hay, wood, and stubble when they stand before the Judgment Seat of Christ.

So be encouraged and inspired to press upward for the prize of the high calling of God in Christ Jesus. In Jesus Name.

GOD MADE YOU

"Being confident of this very thing, that He which hath begun a good work in you will perform it until the day of Jesus Christ." Philippians 1:6

The Lord began a good work in you from birth to present and promises to perform it every day until Jesus returns to earth. In other words, His presence and blessings are a continuous act of God.

Recently, there was a preacher from Africa who said (with a lot of emotion), "Lay your hands on your head every morning and declare a blessing over yourself - - - I am blessed by God, I have His presence on me, I can do all things through Christ who strengthens me, I am loved, I am highly favored, God is for me so who can be against me, the grace of God is on my life," and on and on. Speak the blessings over yourself that come to mind. Then speak the same blessing over your family and your home, your job, your relationships, your finances. This is taking an active part in agreeing with what God is saying to you. You and God agree that you believe what He made you to be.

Now walk every day with the light of Christ shining through your face and heart. Walk with your shoulders back, a smile on your face, and walk tall in your God. He is the Potter; you are the clay, and walk in humility that you are nothing but His hand-picked creation made to give glory to His name.

May His wonderful blessings and unlimited favor and love be upon you. May you make room for the Lord to do greater works. In Jesus Name.

CLOTHED IN BEAUTY

"I will greatly rejoice in the Lord, my soul shall be joyful in my God, for He hath clothed me with the garments of salvation, He hath covered me with the robe of righteousness, as a bridegroom decketh himself with ornaments, and as a bride adorneth herself with her jewels." Isaiah 61:10

"His glory is great in thy salvation: honor and majesty hast thou laid upon Him. For thou hast made him most blessed forever: thou hast made him exceeding glad with thy countenance. For the king trusteth in the Lord, and through the mercy of the Most High he shall not be moved." Psalm 21:5-7

"The blessing of the Lord; it maketh rich, and he addeth no sorrow with it." Proverbs 10:22

God, clothe them with Your beauty and let them be highly favored with breakthrough favor that will open doors of tremendous blessing and opportunities. May the skies part above their heads as You rain down blessings upon them. Visit them with Your Holy Spirit. Lift them up and surround them with holy angels who will minister to them. Use them in Your kingdom purposes to be strong in faith believing God for the impossible. In Jesus Name.

GODLY STRENGTH

The Lord is standing with you ready to bless you to excel in all your endeavors. He asks that you determine in your heart to follow excellence and have the mind of Christ to attain God's fullest desires that He is extending to you. He wants to enrich your life. The higher you go in the Lord the richer your life will be. God has no limits on success. Walk in His presence and the blessings will have no limit. God will multiply beyond measure.

"The Lord God of your fathers make you a thousand times so many more as ye are, and bless you, as He hath promised you." Deuteronomy 1:11

"For You have made him most blessed forever: thou hast made him exceeding glad with thy countenance." Psalm 21:6

May the Lord cause your faith to rise up and take hold of His magnificent blessings. He is a God of miracles. Believe what He says and be a radiant light for Jesus. In Jesus Name.

PRAYER IS EFFECTIVE

God has placed in human hands the mightiest of all forces - PRAYER - so that we might become partners with Him. Prayer always reaches out to others. It should be a rarity that we pray for ourselves, but should always pray in love for those in need.

"The effectual fervent prayer of a righteous man availeth much." James 5:16

God has set us in the strongest relation that binds us, the relation of love, that He may touch one through another in prayer. He binds us together with the ties of love that we may be concerned for each other. If there be but one in a home in touch with God, that one becomes God's door into the whole family. We are most responsible for the ones to whom we are most closely related, i.e. Fathers, Mothers, sisters, and brothers, family, church, friends and the world.

Of all the many important things in life, PRAYER is paramount. Nothing supersedes you spending time in the presence of the Lord.

Jesus prayed this prayer for you:

"Father, I will that they also, whom thou hast given me, be with Me where I am; that they may behold my glory, which thou hast given Me; for thou lovedst Me before the foundation of the world.

"And I have declared unto them thy name, and will declare it: that the love wherewith thou hast loved Me may be in them, and I in them." John 17:24, 26

So may you be marvelously blessed as you also behold the glory of Jesus. Praise Him with all your heart for He is forever worthy. In Jesus Name.

THE BIBLE

Memorizing the Word of God and hiding it in our hearts is a great need in today's world. Let the Bible fill your mind, rule your heart, and guide your life.

"Wherewithal shall a young man cleanse his way? By taking heed thereto according to thy word. With my whole heart have I sought thee: O let me not wander from thy commandments. Thy word have I hid in mine heart, that I might not sin against thee." Psalm 119:9-11

There is little need for memorization because of all the electronic aids that remember our phone numbers, driving directions, and other information we used to learn by repeated use. How many schools are teaching memorization and memory skills?

But in spiritual things, it is good to memorize God's Word. Scripture memory is more than a helpful mental exercise. The goal is to saturate our minds with God's truth so that our minds will conform to His ways. Men in the Bible remembered everything. They exercised their minds constantly.

May you be blessed with a sharp mind to memorize the scriptures and make it a practice to remember things that are needed. May God give you understanding, and wisdom and knowledge of His Word which will change your life. The Word of God is alive. The word was made flesh and dwelt among us. That is Jesus. Jesus is the living Word of God. Be blessed abundantly as you study to show yourself approved of God. In Jesus Name.

AMAZING LOVE

"My little children, let us not love in word, neither in tongue: but in deed and in truth." I John 3:18

When you stand before the Lord, may He say of you that you have loved too many, rather than too few. Love looks beyond what people are to what they can become.

The essence of love is the most comforting and healing of all virtues. When you love someone, you give them trust and assurance. When love is foremost in your life, you become a magnet that people are drawn to. When you are shown love, you are comfortable around that person. There is an ease and a relaxed atmosphere all around. This love seems to give you substance; you are worthy. Love is open arms. Love puts out the "welcome" mat. Love strengthens you and there is a bond with the one you love. Love gives you and the one you love confidence. Love reaches out. Love connects you to others. Love is the nature of God in you. Love needs expression. Love never forgets to express itself. Love believes all things. Love believes in people.

"And we have known and believed the love that God hath to us. God is love; and he that dwelleth in love dwelleth in God, and God in Him." I John 4:16

May the Lord fill your heart with so much love that you will feel complete and confident just because love is there. May you be surrounded with love. May the blessings of the Lord fill your life with those who love you May the Holy Spirit be so alive and real to you that His blessings turn you into a masterpiece for His glory. Love has a wonderful transforming power. In Jesus Name.

PURITY

The stress caused by the issues of life have the potential to create unwanted side effects in your physical body and in your children, family, and even in your animals. Now is the time to deal with the issues and tie up loose ends that keep you from maintaining peace emotionally, mentally and physically. Do not delay in taking care of these matters; procrastination is your enemy. Be diligent to methodically and consistently keep moving towards freedom and tranquility.

God is going to bring you out pure, spotless and undefiled. The blood of Jesus will deliver you of every entanglement and every root that keeps you bound.

"God be merciful unto us, and bless us; and cause His face to shine upon us; that thy way may be known upon earth, thy saving health among all nations. Let the people praise thee, O God; let all the people praise thee. O let the nations be glad and sing for joy: for thou shalt judge the people righteously, and govern the nations upon earth." Psalm 67:1-4

"Then shall the earth yield her increase; and God, even our own God, shall bless us.
God shall bless us; and all the ends of the earth shall fear Him." Psalm 67:6-7

May you feel the Lord's presence. His arms of love are around you. May you honor Him by praying with a thankful heart for the mighty work that He is doing.

Pray intently that God encircle you with angels of protection and you are strengthened to discipline yourself by saying an emphatic "NO" to the wiles and temptations of evil. OVERCOME. In Jesus Name.

OVERCOMER

There is a great truth in the Word of God that is rarely preached or taught, and that is being an "Overcomer." The message is - overcome evil - and when you do, you become an Overcomer, and the powers of the devil do not rule your life or rob you of living a wonderful victorious life. To be overcome by evil is like being overcome by too much wine. You are brought into slavery and mentally disoriented. Evil will rob you of God-given sound reasoning power.

"For if after they have escaped the pollutions of the world through the knowledge of the Lord and Savior Jesus Christ, they are again entangled therein, and overcome, the latter end is worse with them than the beginning.

"For it had been better for them not to have known the way of righteousness, than, after they have known it, to turn from the holy commandment delivered unto them." II Peter 2:20-21

"And the Word of God abideth in you, and ye have overcome the wicked one." I John 2:14

Jesus says, "These things I have spoken unto you, that in Me ye might have peace.

In the world ye shall have tribulation: but be of good cheer; I have overcome the world." John 16:33

Paul says, "Be not overcome of evil, but overcome evil with good." Romans 12:21

John says, "For whatsoever is born of God overcometh the world: and this is the victory that overcometh the world, even our faith. Who is he that overcometh the world, but he that believeth that Jesus is the Son of God?" I John 5:4-5

Overcome evil with good and be abundantly blessed. In Jesus Name.

OVERCOMERS' BLESSNG

Today you can purpose in your mind to be an Overcomer. When you are born of God, you will make a practice of doing what is right at all times and at all cost.

Here is your reward in heaven when you do so:

"Ye are of God, little children, and have overcome them: because greater is he that is in you, than he that is in the world." I John 4:4

"He that hath an ear, let him hear what the Spirit saith unto the churches; To him that overcometh will I give to eat of the tree of life, which is in the midst of the paradise of God."

"He that overcometh shall not be hurt of the second death." (the sinners' death).

"To him that overcometh will I give to eat of the hidden manna, and will give him a white stone, and in the stone a new name written, which no man knoweth saving he that receiveth it.

"He that overcometh, the same shall be clothed in white raiment, and I will not blot out his name out of the book of life, but I will confess his name before my Father, and before his angels." Revelation 2:7, 11, 17; 3:5

You are blessed with strength from the Lord to press through and become a mighty Overcomer. Label yourself as an Overcomer. Speak and declare these scriptures over your life daily. Believe them. You run this race to win. Be blessed as you take the gold. In Jesus Name.

REVIVAL

"For thus saith the high and lofty One that inhabiteth eternity, whose name is Holy; I dwell in the high and holy place, with him also that is of a contrite and humble spirit, to revive the spirit of the humble, and to revive the heart of the contrite ones." Isaiah 57:15

It is the Lord. It is your precious heavenly Father. He is the One who dwells in heaven listening to those who pray with a contrite and humble spirit. It is the Lord who personally revives the spirit of the humble when you call on Him and it is the loving Jesus who revives your heart. That is His promise to you when you pray. When He hears your voice in prayer, you have His full attention to what you are praying. So your time is never wasted when you pray. Talk to Him wherever you are, whether you are walking, sitting, kneeling, lying down, it does not matter. He hears every word you say and will answer every prayer.

"Even them will I bring to My holy mountain, and make them joyful in My house of prayer: for mine house shall be called a house of prayer for all people." Isaiah 56:7

So pray without ceasing, be revived in your spirit and be blessed abundantly.
In Jesus Name.

FOCUS ON THE LORD

The majority of people who fail in this life do so not because of a lack of ability, but due to a lack of *focus*. If you are going to walk successfully with the Lord through this life, and fulfill all His vision for you; then you will find yourself having to say 'no' to far more people and things than those to which you say 'yes'. For you to say 'yes' to everyone and everything all of the time, is for you to be more concerned with being a people-pleaser than a God-pleaser. This will only create for you an approval addiction from people based upon your insecurity in the Lord's love for you, resulting in your attempting to clone yourself into someone or something you are not created to be, in order to meet the shallow, superficial, 'cookie-cutter mold' demands and desires of others. For strait is the gate and narrow is the way that leads to life, and few there *are* who have the focus to find either.

"Enter ye in at the strait gate: for wide is the gate, and broad is the way, that leadeth to destruction, and many there be which go in thereat: Because strait is the gate and narrow is the way, which leadeth unto life, and few there be that find it." Matthew 7:13-14

The reason you were given life is to live - not just exist – not even to exist in the shadow of someone else. Fullness of life is to live in obedience to the Lord and be conformed into His image. He is life and in Him is joy unspeakable and full of glory. Your life will turn around when you fully follow Jesus and a wonderful door of huge blessings will open up to you, more than you ever expected.

"But this one thing I do, forgetting those things which are behind, and reaching forth unto those things which are before. I press toward the mark for the prize of the high calling of God in Christ Jesus." Philippians 3:13-14

Focus on Jesus and live your life as one called out from the crowd to join in oneness to Him, and be gloriously blessed. In Jesus Name.

ROAD LESS TRAVELED

To attain to the highest goals in life requires change, almost daily change. God's Spirit alters your atmosphere. The ordinary, the commonplace, the crowd, always follows the road most traveled where the worldly live. What are your goals? Where are your aspirations leading you? Are they worldly? Or are they spiritual? What you choose will determine how strong you will be spiritually. By choosing a worldly life you will lose your way with God. To remain true to the Lord reveals the strength of your character. It does not take effort to drift with the tides of the world. But to walk with the Lord requires strong determination.

So may you shine like the brightest star, walk with dignity and class and not crass, living your life to the fullest. May God promote you and cause you to excel above your expectations. May you shine in the darkest places where it is impossible to love. May God protect you at all times, lifting you up in His arms of safety, knowing that when you walk with the Lord you are always safe and secure.

God says, "I will heal their backsliding; I will love them freely: for mine anger is turned away from him." Hosea 14:4

In Jesus Name.

INTERESTING BIBLE

A number of scientists and Biblical scholars have written about statistical probabilities of prophesies in the Bible. The probability of the chance fulfillment of thirteen Bible predictions/prophesies about specific people and their specific actions showed less than one chance in $10/^{138}$ that such predictions/prophesies could come to pass without the supernatural intervention of God. That means less than one chance in 10 with 138 zeros following.

Biblical prophecy is not theoretical. It was spoken by Almighty God, and they all came true through Christ. Jesus fulfilled all prophecy that was ever spoken in the Bible. For any one man to fulfill 48 prophesies would be the chance of one in $10/^{157}$. That means 10 with 157 zeros following.

"Think not that I am come to destroy the law, or the prophets; I am not come to destroy, but to fulfill. For verily I say unto you, Till heaven and earth pass, one jot or one tittle shall in no wise pass from the law, till all be fulfilled." Matthew 5:17-18

The Bible was written in the Hebrew language and one word is built upon another word. Every letter has seven meanings and every word has 70 meanings. Every dot and tittle in the Hebrew language has a meaning and if just one were left out, it would entirely change the meaning of the word. So the specificity of the dot and tittle is very important.

"Study to show thyself approved unto God, a workman that needeth not to be ashamed, rightly dividing the word of truth." II Timothy 2:15

"All scripture is given by inspiration of God, and is profitable for doctrine, for reproof, for correction, for instruction in righteousness; That the man of God may be perfect, thoroughly furnished unto all good works." II Timothy 3:16-17

Your Bible is the most important book in the world. All knowledge is contained in your Bible. Be blessed as you read and study it. In Jesus Name.

ABOVE IT ALL

May the hand of the Lord be stretched out to you as He fills you with His virtue, miraculous power, ability, abundance, stamina, strength, and mighty power. May God dispatch angels to stand beside you, around you, and encircle all that is yours, so no evil power comes near you. The enemy cannot penetrate the wall of protection that the Lord has put around you, and is mad and frustrated because he cannot get to you. This only attests to your victory and his defeat. Stand tall. You are in the midst of holiness.

Christ in you jumps every hurdle and opens the way for you to be you, the one who is fashioned in the image of Jesus, having love as the very essence of your being. He will bring you to run the Christian race and successfully cross the finish line in full array of what He purposed since the foundation of the world. Every act of God toward you is a blessing. It is solid and is established with the end result in mind. He sees it all. Take confidence in Him.

"And we know that all things work together for good to them that love God, to them who are the called according to his purpose." Romans 8:28

May you walk not after the flesh but after the Spirit. May the Holy Spirit stand armed and ready to defend you and bring you safely into the harbor of God. May He refresh your soul by breathing new life into your lungs. He will cup His hands under your feet and lift you above the thunderous maze around the earth. There is a higher place where light is not deflected by darkness. That is where the Lord is lifting you into heavenly realms, where you are rightfully seated with Christ. In Jesus Name.

LOOK UP

Lord, scatter the enemy by Your power and let today be free from clutter and anxiety that disturbs the mind to struggle with issues. Speak peace and quietness of heart over all my family and readers so they can relax and come into total trust in Jesus. In Jesus Name.

Narrow all your interests until the attitude of mind, soul, heart, spirit and body is concentration on Jesus. He is your source of help. He takes all the troublesome cares of life upon Himself and bears all your burdens. It is the Lord who is your protection and lifts your soul to stand tall with the strength of God coursing through every vessel of your body. He is mighty to save. He is mighty to heal. He is mighty to walk ahead of you and parts the way. All rubbish of the world and its nature is removed and you are cleansed by the blood of the Lamb. Walk in confidence, with assurance of heart, for the Lord is surely with you to guide you in truth.

"For I know the thoughts that I think toward you, saith the Lord, thoughts of peace, and not of evil, to give you an expected end. Then shall ye call upon Me, and ye shall go and pray unto me, and I will hearken unto you. And ye shall seek Me, and find Me, when ye shall search for Me with all your heart." Jeremiah 29:11-13

What was bound yesterday is loosed today. What was discouraging yesterday is taken off you today. Your distorted future is cleansed and made clear by the blood of Jesus. What looked impossible yesterday is subject to the word of God that, "All things are possible to them who believe." Everything that has been put on you by the enemy is removed by the blood of Jesus and you are free. That weight was never yours to carry.

May the blessings of the Lord come into your soul and give you peace. In Jesus Name.

MAN'S WAYS ARE PLEASING

May the joy of the Lord be your strength, and His righteousness fill the very air around you. You belong to a holy God who wants to fill your world with favor and liveliness, which means a life full of vigor, spirited, brilliant, quick to rebound, vivacious, keenly alive, alert, attractive with gaiety, and quickness of gesture and wit. May your heart be filled with laughter and happiness. May you be blessed with lightheartedness and freedom to rejoice for all the good things God has done for you. Do you have eyesight? It's a gift. Do you have a good mind? It's a gift. Are you healthy? That's a gift. Do you have leadership abilities that cause others to follow? These are all gifts. Has God blessed you with a family? Has He given you sufficient clothes? These are all gifts from God's hand. Reflect on His numerous gifts to you. It will increase your joy

"Blessed is the nation whose God is the Lord; and the people whom He hath chosen for His own inheritance." Psalm 33:12

May your life be full of God's goodness and His bountiful blessings. You are chosen as the Lord's own inheritance throughout eternity. In Jesus Name.

OBEDIENCE PAYS

The Lord never overlooks our obedience to Him. When He says something and we obey, by our obedience God swings open the door to more blessings than you can contain. Here are just two examples: If you tithe and give offerings on the money you have, God pronounces tremendous blessings upon you. The following is an awesome scripture to claim:

"Bring ye all the tithes into the storehouse, that there may be meat in my house, and prove me now herewith, saith the Lord of hosts, if I will not open you the windows of heaven, and pour you out a blessing, that there shall not be room enough to receive it.

"And I will rebuke the devourer for your sakes, and he shall not destroy the fruits of your ground; neither shall your vine cast her fruit before the time in the field, saith the Lord of hosts.

"And all nations shall call you blessed: for you shall be a delight-some land, saith the Lord of hosts." Malachi 3:10-12

There was a man in the Bible called Jonadab who told his children, "Drink no wine," and all the generations that followed obeyed and none drank wine.

Because of their obedience to their father, God promised them that "they shall not want a man to stand before Him forever." That meant that all his family would walk with the Lord forever, generation after generation.

These are only two examples of the tremendous blessings that come through obedience to God. He is the sovereign power and knows all things. He knows what is best for you and asks only that you follow Him in obedience. He has given you direction in the Bible and promises that He will fulfill as you walk in obedience to Him.

May God fill your day with His wonderful blessings and you consistently draw closer to Him. Pray and you will be amazed how quickly He answers. Be blessed precious ones. In Jesus Name.

PRESS INTO GOD

This morning, the thought of the greatness of God was awe-inspiring. The extent of His power has never been discovered. It reaches into the highest heights and into the smallest places. He is God over all. And He holds you in the hollow of His hands. Within your heart is Christ. You were formed by God. The great I AM is the Lord your God.

"I have made the earth, and created man upon it: I, even my hands, have stretched out the heavens, and all their host have I commanded.

"I have raised him up in righteousness, and I will direct all his ways: he shall build my city, and he shall let go my captives, not for price nor reward, saith the Lord of hosts.

"Look unto me, and be ye saved, all the ends of the earth: for I am God, and there is none else." Isaiah 45:12, 13, 22

May your heart hunger and thirst for righteousness. May it be you desire to press into God and let Him enfold you in His arms of holiness, peace, healing and comfort. He wants to impart to you more of His character and virtue and integrity. The blessings are limitless as you draw near to Him in righteousness.

May you lift up your hands to a holy God who will strengthen and cleanse you. He will surround your life with those who love you, who appreciate you and validate who you really are, the person God made you to be. You are an awesome, wonderful creation of the Lord. Ask God to reveal to you who you really are. He has even called you by your name. He knows you. May He fill your heart with the light of God and drive out all darkness. May you reach up your hands to the Lord. He will meet you there. In Jesus Name.

CHOOSE NO EVIL

May you desire the Lord to cleanse even the atmosphere around you. May you only choose to go places where the Christ in you would be welcome. May you choose not to hear blasphemy or evil speaking, but choose to walk in a high level of integrity. You are called to be holy for you carry a Holy Jesus in your heart and this empowers you to have a special anointing to overcome any evil that you may be tempted with.

"I am the Lord your God, which have separated you from other people. And ye shall be holy unto Me: for I the Lord am holy, and have severed you from other people, that ye should be mine." Leviticus 20:24, 26

It is God, "Who has saved us, and called us with a holy calling, not according to our works, but according to His own purpose and grace, which was given us in Christ Jesus before the world began." II Timothy 1:9

"Be not overcome of evil, but overcome evil with good." Romans 12:21

May the wonderful blessings of God's light shine into your heart and soul and bring a whole new awareness of the glorious blessings He has in store for you.

In Jesus Name.

HONESTY AND HUMILITY

Picture a bowling alley. If the ball goes too far to the right or left, it will wind up in the gutter and be wasted. But if the ball goes down the middle, it will knock all the pins down and score a ten. The lane is clear. No pins are still standing. If the ball goes a little to the left or right, a few pins will be knocked down and a few still standing.

The ball is you, the pins are sinful obstacles along the way, and the center of the lane is the path where God leads you.

This is an analogy of the Christian walk. When you walk with the Lord in the center of the road, becoming more Christ-like, maintaining His godly attributes and character, living to yield yourselves to Him and walk in obedience to His Word, you receive the shield of honor from the Lord. You walk in all His blessings and wherever you go, you carry the presence of the Lord with you.

"For the Lord God is a sun and shield: the Lord will give grace and glory: no good thing will He withhold from them that walk uprightly.
O Lord of hosts, blessed is the man that trusteth in thee." Psalm 84:11-12

"Honor shall uphold the humble in spirit." Proverbs 29:23

May the blessings of the Most High God be very effective in your life and you are transformed daily. May you seek out godly leaders who carry a holy mantle of the Holy Spirit and stay close to them, stay under godly teaching, be healed from the top of your head to the soles of your feet and be made whole. In Jesus Name.

POWER OF PRAYER

Every prayer that Paul and all the disciples prayed are still being answered, even those in the Old Testament. In Revelation 5:8, it says there are golden vials full of odors which are the prayers of saints. Odors mean fragrant, aromatic fumes that ascend up to the Father in heaven and prayers never dissipate, but are held in golden vials. Prayer is powerful. Your greatest ministry will be on your knees praying before God in the name of Jesus. Then the one for whom you prayed is touched by the Holy Spirit as He moves to fulfill what was prayed. Distance from the one for whom you pray matters not, for your prayers go up to God and it is He who moves to fulfill them. You can only pray in the will of God as His Spirit prays through you. Listen to Him and pray.

Cornelius was a centurion in Caesarea who was visited by an angel of God who stood before him in bright clothing and said, "Cornelius, thy prayer is heard, and thine alms are had in remembrance in the sight of God." From this encounter he sent for Peter, who was told by God that He is no respecter of persons, because that on the Gentiles also was poured out the gift of the Holy Spirit, as had been given to the Jew. Through Cornelius' prayers the division between Jew and Gentile was severed.

Anna was an 84-year old widow, who was a prophetess, which departed not from the temple, but served God with fasting and prayer night and day. She instantly came into the temple when Jesus was brought in as a baby and the minute she saw Him she knew He was the Messiah, the Savior of the world.

"If my people, which are called by My name, shall humble themselves, and pray, and seek my face, and turn from their wicked ways; then will I hear from heaven, and will forgive their sin, and will heal their land." II Chronicles 7:14

May you be blessed by the many prayers that have been prayed for you, that are continually working in your life by the Holy Spirit to fulfill God's perfect will. May you yield your all to Him. He will do through you great and mighty works by faith that will bring many souls into the kingdom of God.
In Jesus Name.

GOD'S TIMING FOR PRAYER

Sometimes God sees something going on in the earth that needs to be prayed for. God is in heaven and He sees everything. On such an occasion, the Lord said, "Go pray." A missionary in Tunis, Tunisia needed prayer. So while praying, the Lord took me into His presence and said, "Look back." As I turned to my left, I looked in the far distance and saw the earth that appeared the size of a jack ball. When we were young, we played jacks with a ball smaller than a golf ball. After seeing the earth, I turned to the Lord, and He said, "Is anything too hard for Me?"

Since that day, I have never doubted God.

Six weeks later, the missionary from Tunis came to a missionary convention at our church and I told her of the call to pray and asked, "Do you remember what was happening about six weeks ago?" She said, "Oh yes. My husband, who that day became enraged and began beating me. I fell to the floor and he continued beating me and I feared for my life that he was going to beat me until he killed me. But suddenly he stopped, stood over me and said, 'Get out of here. I hate you and never want to see you again.' After gathering up what I could, I left and flew back to the States."

"Praying always with all prayer and supplication in the Spirit, and watching thereunto with all perseverance and supplication for all saints." Ephesians 6:18

May the blessings of peace, love, faith, grace and anointing of the Holy Spirit be upon you as doors of glory open before your very eyes and you see exactly what the Lord had in mind all the time. In Jesus Name.

THE LORD'S RETURN

"For the Lord Himself shall descend from heaven with a shout, with the voice of the archangel, and with the trump of God: and the dead in Christ shall rise first: then we which are alive and remain shall be caught up together with them in the clouds, to meet the Lord in the air: and so shall we ever be with the Lord. Wherefore comfort one another with these words." I Thessalonians 4:16-17

You are so blessed for one day you shall see Jesus coming in the clouds of heaven with power and great glory. This is your hope. This is your comfort.

Having studied the book of Revelation and science, Nostradamus and Isaac Newton believe the Lord could return as early as 2012 or 2016. The Bible says no man knows the day nor the hour but God only. Jesus tells us to "take heed" and watch the signs going on around you.

Father, we ask that all your children be spiritually prepared and ready for the return of Jesus, and be as children of light, and children of the day. They are not of the night, nor of darkness. For we know full well that the day of the Lord so comes as a thief in the night. We ask, Lord, that they not be lulled to sleep and be as the world.

"But let us who are of the day, be sober, putting on the breastplate of faith, and love; and for a helmet, the hope of salvation. For God hath not appointed us to wrath, but to obtain salvation by our Lord Jesus Christ, Who died for us, that, whether we wake or sleep, we should live together with Him. Wherefore, comfort yourselves together, and edify one another, even as also you do." I Thessalonians 5:8-11

May you be abundantly blessed of the Lord, rejoicing evermore, praying without ceasing, warn them that are unruly, comfort the feeble-minded, support the weak, be patient toward all men. See that none render evil for evil unto any man; but ever follow that which is good, both among yourselves, and to all men. In Jesus Name.

"In everything give thanks: for this is the will of God in Christ Jesus concerning you.
Quench not the Spirit. Despise not prophesying. Prove all things; hold fast that which is good. Abstain from all appearance of evil.

And the very God of peace sanctify you wholly; and I pray God your whole spirit and soul and body be preserved blameless unto the coming of our Lord Jesus Christ.

Faithful is He that called you, who also will do it." I Thessalonians 5:18-24

LaVergne, TN USA
14 November 2010
204842LV00004B/2/P